PECULIAR SPEECH

Peculiar Speech

Preaching to the Baptized

William H. Willimon

William B. Eerdmans Publishing Company
Grand Rapids, Michigan

Copyright © 1992 by Wm. B. Eerdmans Publishing Co.
255 Jefferson Ave. S.E., Grand Rapids, Mich. 49503
All rights reserved
Reprinted, December 1992
Printed in the United States of America

Library of Congress Cataloging-in-Publication Data

Willimon, William H.
Peculiar speech: preaching to the baptized / William H. Willimon.
p.   cm.
ISBN 0-8028-0616-3
1. Preaching. 2. Baptism. 3. Sermons, American. I. Title.
BV4211.2.W53   1992
251 — dc20   92-4735
CIP

To
Walter Brueggemann
in gratitude

Contents

Preface

THIS book began as a suggestion that grew into an exposition. That is often the way it is with us preachers. Give us one forlorn carnation and enough time, and we will work it up into a bridal bouquet.

Walter Brueggemann said that he was tired of sermons that address no one in particular, least of all those who have been baptized. That got me thinking. Here I am in a university chapel. The temptation to speak to the "general human condition" is almost unavoidable. We are even more susceptible to the temptation to believe that here at the university we actually know what is the "general human condition." How many of our sermons speak as if no one in particular has gathered here, as if we are an audience of disinterested listeners, as if nothing like life or death were at stake in our speech? Such speaking is an affront to the dignity of the baptized.

The baptized gather here on Sunday because they have been called, summoned. They are not here because of a vague curiosity about the "human condition." Other entities presume to address that state — in a way, I might add, much less threatening than the approach represented by the church.

They are not here to be titillated, entertained, or even reassured. If all they want is entertainment, let them fly to Vegas. If mere reassurance can soothe their pain, a score of chemicals and self-help books are cheaper than church. Leo Buscaglia us all over.

No. The baptized congregate because they have been called. *I* certainly did not call them. If *I* were calling a church, I doubt that I would have called *this* church. I am, I have noted over the years, a good deal more discriminating than God.

So last Sunday, when someone emerged from the church door, at the end of the service, steamed up over my associate's sermon, I could say, "I know Ms. Ferree-Clark personally. I have worked with her for seven years now. She is an unfailingly sweet and gracious person, someone who does not relish conflict nor provoke anger. If her sermon has upset you, your anger cannot be blamed on her. No, I detect the work of someone else behind this sermon, someone a good deal more at home with confrontation and conflict than either Ms. Ferree-Clark or I. Perhaps he is the one to whom you should make your complaint. After all, neither my associate nor I called you here this morning. The material we preach did not originate with us."

I hope that my pastoral impertinence reminded this person of how odd it is (and at times discomforting) to be a disciple.

This book took shape out of a series of lectures at The Austin Presbyterian Seminary, Austin, Texas, in 1991. The response to my lectures prompted me to put these thoughts into print. M. Richard Niebuhr, whose *Christ and Culture* is criticized in this book, delivered *Christ and Culture* as lectures at Austin Presbyterian Seminary in 1949. Although neither I nor my work is equal in significance to the life and work of that great Christian, some may feel that this book signals for American Christians a definite turn in the road much traveled since Niebuhr.

To my son, William Parker, and my daughter, Harriet

Patricia, whose baptisms were about the best moments in my life, I dedicate this work.

Duke University Chapel   William H. Willimon
Pentecost, 1991

1

Preaching as Baptismal Speech

Eternal Father:
When nothing existed but chaos,
   you swept across the dark waters
   and brought forth light.
In the days of Noah,
   you saved those on the ark through water.
After the flood you set in the clouds a rainbow.
When you saw your people as slaves in Egypt,
   you led them to freedom through the sea. . . .
In the fullness of time you sent Jesus,
   nurtured in the water of a womb.
He was baptized by John and anointed by your Spirit.
He called his disciples
   to share in the baptism of his death and resurrection
   and to make disciples of all nations.

> (From the "Thanksgiving Over the Water,"
> *The United Methodist Hymnal,* p. 36)

I WANT to look at preaching through baptism. The preacher is the one who, in service to the church, strikes the rock and brings forth water in dry places.

In Egypt, we thought our problem was our need for liberation. But once liberated, free, we were thirsty; at least Pharaoh gave us water and three square meals a day. And we murmured against Moses, asking, "Why did you bring us out of Egypt, to kill us and our children . . . with thirst?" (Exodus 17:3). Slavery began to look good. Most of the really stupid things we have done in our history are attributable to our seemingly unquenchable thirst.

And Moses asked, "What shall I do with this people? They are almost ready to stone me" (Exodus 17:4). And Yahweh told Moses to take the rod, the same with which he struck the Nile, and strike the rock at Horeb. And Moses did so, and there was water. And Moses named the place, among other things, Massah because there, in water, the people received response to their question, "Is the LORD among us or not?" (17:7).

Whenever we gather on Sunday, that is still our question. Is the Lord among us or not? We thought that our problem was our need for freedom, for liberation. No. Our problem is thirst. Our controversy is over appropriate ways to quench thirst. And every Sunday the preacher strikes the rock and there is water, things are brought to speech, and silence is broken. The Lord is with us.

In his book *Homiletic,* David Buttrick notes how a preacher's speech will be determined, to a great extent, by how the preacher defines the congregation to which the sermon is addressed. Buttrick characterizes the congregation as having a "double consciousness":

> On a Sunday morning congregations are constituted in liturgy as "people of God" and, in fact, within the symbolic structures of liturgy understand themselves so constituted.

At the same time, we know we are "in the world" and share worldly ways of understanding. Thus, because we are "*in* but not *of* the world," preaching will have to speak to a double consciousness. Theological reality is primary, thus preaching will be explication, a "bringing into view" of our common faith. At the same time, because awareness of being-saved involves a distinguishing of Christian faith from understandings of the world-age in which we live, the language of preaching will wrestle with ideas, assumptions, social attitudes which we bring to church. If preaching does involve conversion, it is the constant conversion of Christian formation. In a worldly language, preaching shapes the faith-consciousness of the church.[1]

Much of the preaching I hear, and much that I do, appears to be more aware of the second aspect of Buttrick's doubly conscious congregation. We speak as if we were speaking only to people in the world. Our "worldly language" doesn't produce Christian formation. In this book, I want to explore what it means to preach on Sunday amid the baptized. *What difference does it make to our preaching that all of us there are either preparing for baptism or else trying to figure out what happened when we were baptized?* Either the listeners have already accepted this radical, peculiar, distinctive identity and vocation or they are being invited to do so. We preach either under the promise of baptism, "Come forth, be washed, and you shall be odd," or the mandate of baptism, "You are washed, you are ordained, you are odd." Do we preachers appreciate the baptismal, liturgical quality of our speech?

1. David Buttrick, *Homiletic: Moves and Structures* (Philadelphia: Fortress, 1987), p. 41.

3

Distinctive Discourse

It has long been said by the church that, because worship is an act of the church, and because the church is before all else a community at worship before God in Christ, worship precedes theological reflection and subordinates it. Worship is not an "authority" or "source for theology"; it is the ontological condition of theology, the font out of which proper understanding of the *kerygma* (proclamation) arises. This was expressed in the old patristic position, *Legem credendi lex statuat supplicandi*. (The law of prayer precedes the law of belief.)

The church's worship is nothing other than the church's faith in motion, both in its most sublime and on its most practical levels. The worship of a church does not merely reflect the church's faith but actualizes it concretely in a sustained manner across the generations and in an irreducible way. Worship is the scripture's home rather than its stepchild. The Bible is the church's first liturgical book. Preaching is best conceived of as an act of worship, the precedent of and a commentary upon baptism.

To speak among the baptized, those who are dying and being raised (Romans 6:4), is to enter into a world of odd communication and peculiar speech. Baptismal speech need not conform to the reasons of this world (Romans 12:2). Conversation among the baptized is ecclesial in nature, political. A peculiar *polis* is being formed here, a family, a holy nation, a new people where once there was none (the images are all baptismal, 1 Peter 2:9).

Forgetting the baptismal context of our preaching, we risk distorting the gospel into an intellectual dilemma: how can modern, twentieth-century people believe a first-century Jew? It becomes a matter of subjective affirmation ("this seems right to me"), or of nodding whenever our particular gender, racial, or cultural button is pushed. But the gospel is none of these.

4

Rather, in baptism, we are subsumed into a story of water and the word. A story of creation formed out of dark waters. A story of a God so righteous that he was willing to make war on the world he created, only to hang up his bow and to promise never to give up on us again. A story of a people, created out of nothing, by a God determined to be worshipped rightly, led through waters into the desert as imperial chariots foundered. A story of a Jewish woman visited by God in a way that confounded her fiancé but caused her to sing. A story of a crazy man out in the desert proclaiming a new kingdom coming in water and fire. A story of one who saved by an issue of water and blood.

As Augustine noted, water is water. "The word is added to the element, and there results the Sacrament, as if itself also a kind of visible word." Water set next to the word, next to *this* story, is called baptism. Luther, following Augustine, emphasized that baptism "is not merely water, but water used according to God's command and connected with God's word."

Christian preaching brings out or brings into view the mystery inherent in the waters of baptism. Baptismal preaching names the reality to which we have all been exposed, that is, the peculiar salvation of this crucified God. Therefore baptismal preaching is not so much a matter of being didactic, of explaining something, as it is of testifying to something, struggling to describe an event that has already happened to the congregation, bringing into view the significance of our baptism with words.

The theology of the church is the church's attempt to speak of the change wrought in itself through baptism. As Thomas C. Oden has said, "Christian theology fundamentally began as a lengthy set of footnotes on the baptismal formula which preceded all deliberate Christian doctrinal formulation. All the heresies against which early pastoral care had to struggle were essentially offenses against the baptismal formula."[2]

One of the reasons why "the language of preaching is essentially metaphorical"[3] is not just that people enjoy the use of metaphor but rather that an act like baptism sets the tone and determines the mode for Christian communication. Speech must fit that which it attempts to describe.

To preach among the baptized or the being baptized is to operate within *a domain of distinctive discourse.* We talk differently here, work within a certain "language game" to which everyone here subscribes for the duration of the conversation. The language is rooted in the elemental narrative testimony: "Do you not know that all of us who have been baptized into Christ Jesus were baptized into his death? Therefore we have been buried with him by baptism into death, so that, just as Christ was raised from the dead by the glory of the Father, so we too might walk in newness of life" (Romans 6:3-4).

A distinctive identity arises from this distinctive community of discourse. There is politics in our preaching. I am troubled by preaching that won't come clean on its politics. We speak of expository preaching, or narrative preaching, story preaching, inductive, deductive preaching as if preaching were mainly a matter of method, of style, as if nothing political were at stake in the mode of our communication, as if no particular people were congregating due to our speaking, as if being Christian were synonymous with being a good human being who speaks conventional imperial English but with a certain accent.

No matter our style of preaching, there is no way for us preachers to weasel out of the baptismal truth that we preach within a distinctive universe of discourse. We talk funny.

2. Thomas C. Oden, *Ministry through Word and Sacrament* (New York: Crossroad, 1989), p. 110.
3. Buttrick, p. 125.

Last fall we had a panel discussion on "Homosexuality and the Church." (Who told us to call people "homosexual"? A nineteenth-century Viennese psychotherapist who wrote a book arguing that there were males, females, and a third sex, homosexuals. What on earth are we talking about when we talk this way? Why would the church be interested in such labeling of people?) After the discussion, a young man came up to me saying that he was "a baptized Episcopalian" and "none of you have a right to tell me who I am. I define myself."

I noted that if his first declaration were true ("I am a baptized Episcopalian"), his second was false. In baptizing this young man the church was quite clear, or at least should have been clear (false advertising is so wrong), that we were telling him who he was, namely a cherished child of God who was washed, gifted, chosen, called, and named.

Not knowing who names us is a tragic plight. The uncalled life is an empty one. Identity is too important a matter to be left to individuals. Why we believe this to be true requires the telling of a story that is baptismal.

Our speech becomes corrupted, not only by Viennese psychotherapists but also in church assemblies. What are we to do with a church that speaks to people on the basis of their gender or race, all the while baptizing them on the basis of Galatians 3:28? "Before faith came, we were confined under the law, kept under restraint. . . . But now that faith has come, we are no longer under a custodian. . . . For as many of you as were baptized into Christ have put on Christ. There is neither Jew nor Greek, there is neither slave nor free, there is neither male nor female; for you are all one in Christ Jesus" (Galatians 3:23, 25, 27-28, RSV).

When Christians are invited to say something about social justice, we begin by saying "church," which is to say "baptism": "For indeed we were all brought into one body by baptism, in the one Spirit, whether we are Jews or Greeks, whether slaves or free, and that one Holy Spirit was poured out for all of us to drink" (1 Corinthians 12:13, NEB). Poured out for *all* to drink, no matter race, gender, class, or sexual orientation. "Now that faith has come" (Galatians 3:25) we speak differently to one another than when we were kept under restraint by the custodian of quotas, gender issues, and ethnic pride.

In the words of John Alsup, by these baptismal texts "we are invited to imagine the New as life in the flesh where the latter is not the dominant reality for the people of faith."[4] In baptism, it is not so much that worldly labels like race or gender are washed away as that we recapitulate creation and become new as if in the primal waters of creation, dying to our old selves and rising to newness of life.

We preachers need not be embarrassed by the distinctiveness of our speech. It is rooted in primordial narrative. "The sea roared," "the wind of God moved over the face of the waters" (Genesis 1:2). "The waters prevailed. . . . everything on the dry land in whose nostrils was the breath of life died" (Genesis 7:20, 22, RSV).

At the university, when we attempt to address the factors that divide us we must rely on language speaking of "multiculturalism," or "the value of diversity," or "pluralism" in an attempt to put a happy face on our fragmentation. Though such speech is devoid of power to transform or even adequately to describe the depth of our divisions it's the best we can do at a place like the university, which knows not the baptismal phenomenon behind Galatians 3. You stay out of my "culture" and I'll stay out of yours. We call it "tolerance," but it is another name for loneliness.

So the preacher need not always be looking over her shoulder, justifying pulpit rhetoric according to some other

4. John Alsup, "Imagining the New: Feminism, Galatians 3:28 and the Current Interpretive Discussion," *Austin Seminary Review,* pp. 92-108.

criterion. Lacking confidence in the power of our story to effect that of which it speaks, to evoke a new people out of nothing, our communication loses its nerve. Nothing is said that could not be heard elsewhere, nobody need die and be raised to assimilate the speech of the Empire or its universities.

Unfortunately, most of the theology I learned in seminary was in the translation mode. Take this biblical image and translate it into something more palatable to people who use Cuisinarts. The modern church has been willing to use everyone's language but its own. In conservative contexts, gospel speech is traded for dogmatic assertion and moralism, for self-help psychologies and narcotic mantras. In more liberal speech, talk tiptoes around the outrage of Christian discourse and ends up as an innocuous, though urbane, affirmation of the ruling order. Unable to preach Christ and him crucified, we preach humanity and it improved. As Walter Brueggemann said, when the preacher is uncertain about speech, a great deal of energy is expended reassuring the listener that nothing will be said that would require conversion in order to be understood, certainly nothing that would be regarded by cultured despisers as either foolish or weak. By the time most of us finish qualifying the scandal of Christian speech, very little can be said by the preacher that can't be heard elsewhere.

To categorize preaching as distinctive baptismal speech is to part company with advocates of linguistic accommodation like David Tracy, who argues (in his books like *Plurality and Ambiguity*) that our speech must bow to what he calls "public criteria." Tracy says, "the demand for public criteria for truth-claims remains both the initial impetus and the great hope for all contemporary theology."[5] He is surely right about the desire for "public speech" as the great hope of contemporary

5. David Tracy, *The Christian Century*, Oct. 10, 1990, p. 901.

theology.[6] Yet Tracy is surely wrong in his claim that when ecclesial speech takes its own distinctiveness seriously it becomes private and introverted in a way in which Tracy's speech is not. Tracy claims to fight "obscurantism" and "mystification" — two terms not used by too wide a "public," I daresay. In reality his is the privileged talk of the academy, and one branch of the fragmented academy at that. All energy is expended upon consideration of method as if we could find a method of talking that would enable us to bypass having to admit that, as Christians (or as university professors), our talk arises out of our account of the world, out of a story that is not universal.

So when Tracy speaks of the need to defend "reason" he acts as if there really is some innate, noncontingent, universal human attribute called "reason" as opposed to contingent, story-dependent activities like baptismal speech. No. Tracy's "reason" is a way of talking about the world in the hope that our communities, our traditions, our stories don't matter. (If that were true, why doesn't Tracy's reason sound more "reasonable" outside the confines of The University of Chicago?) We keep hoping that we could find some universal speech, some universal, contextless attribute like "reason" that would enable us to organize the world without having to take our differences seriously.

When Christians are asked to say something "reasonable," we say something like, "Repent!" or "Join Up," or "You must be born again." Why we speak thus is rationality that can only be understood by reference to a story that is baptismal. We must not degrade those who misunderstand us by claiming that they are dumb or unreasonable. They simply have not yet heard the story that makes our Christian speech intelligible.

Baptismal speech is every bit as "public" as Tracy's Chicago

6. Cf. Thomas C. Oden, *After Modernity . . . What?* (Grand Rapids: Zondervan, 1990).

"analogic imagination." It's just that, when we talk in public, we Christians expect to be honest about the narrative, communal basis of our speech, whereas most advocates of "reason" do not. Baptismal speaking reminds us that very little speech makes sense apart from a narrative and a community that makes it make sense.[7]

The Authoritative Text

Baptismal preaching recognizes the canonical text as norm. We live or die, as God's new people, by our ability to listen to these texts without killing the preacher for speaking them. Not that we all agree on the hermeneutics of these texts. We all agree to listen, expecting to be surprised by what we hear because we expect to hear the living God speak through these texts. Our listening is therefore an act of faith, faith that the Holy Spirit really is active, that it enlivens these texts to be for us the word that gives life, water in dry places, so we cannot listen "objectively" (pace older historical criticism). We are never neutral with these texts because we listen expecting these texts to form a community that would not be here without these texts. This is our epistemological bias, the vested interest that informs our listening to these texts. We listen as church, as the baptized and still being baptized. (How well Elizabeth Schüssler Fiorenza has demonstrated the reality and unavoidability of our epistemological biases in reading Scripture in her *Bread Not Stone*.)[8] So we are not saying that it is possible or desirable to read the Bible without vested interest. We are saying that the Bible ought to be read with interests appropriate to biblical creation and purposes.

7. Cf. Gerhard Lohfink, *Jesus and Community: The Social Dimension of the Christian Faith* (Philadelphia: Fortress, 1984).
8. Elizabeth Schüssler Fiorenza, *Bread Not Stone* (Boston: Beacon, 1984).

The text itself also has a vested interest, namely *to create and to critique a new people.*

There is power in preaching from the canonical text. That's why there are few things more important for a preacher than to preach from the Common Lectionary. Most of our people are under the impression that we preach what's on our mind. They say, "Well, he's often a bag of hot air, but he visited Mama this week in the hospital, so we allow him twenty to thirty minutes to vent his political opinions each week in exchange for his being so nice." ("He's full of hot air, but he's *our* hot air.")

No. In preaching from the Lectionary, we demonstrate that we preach what we have been *told.* We make visible that our preaching is the result of our having borne the burden of the church's book. We make clear our authority. This is great grace for us preachers. Then, when they say they don't like something we've said, we can say, "Don't tell me. It's not *my* book. *I* didn't call you forth to listen. Don't complain to me."

As I heard Walter Brueggemann say to us preachers, "If you are a coward by nature, if boldness does not come to you naturally, then you can get down and hide behind the text. You can peek out from behind the text. You can say, 'It's not me saying this. It's the text!'"

Or more to the point, Elizabeth Achtemeier says, "As preacher your job is to preach the text, not apologize for it." In fact, in baptism, we ought to dispose of the whole notion of "the text," as if the Bible were bits and pieces of ancient, sometimes interesting information. "The text" implies that the Bible has some sort of independent status apart from that community that created the Bible and is in turn re-created by it. One does not know the meaning of these texts without inquiring into the community that is being formed by these texts. In baptism, the text becomes Scripture for us, canon, laid on us as a new story that illumines our stories. In baptism we are adopted into the people who answer to this story and are held accountable to its description of reality. In baptism we are not free to go searching for better texts, the canon of Freud, Adam Smith, or Alice Walker. The term "text" suggests to me another means of vesting authority in ourselves and our use of Scripture. "Scripture" suggests that authority has shifted from ourselves to Scripture's use of us.

When the text is not authoritative, the preacher's speech is in jeopardy and we have nowhere to stand. Inadequate ecclesiology is often at the bottom of our ineffective hermeneutics. The Scripture is not just text, it is Scripture, canon. Baptism asserts that we meet and speak under an identity that challenges and endangers all other identities. The texts from which we must preach have few epistemological allies in the world. They cannot be easily translated, transposed into our psychological, sociological speech.

Most of my preaching founders when I ignore the ecclesiological (that is, political) context of preaching and I grope for a credible point of contact with my listening congregation somewhere other than the normative canon. Where baptismal identity is lacking, listening is done from a cultural context — usually the therapeutic — other than that of the counter-cultural community called church,

Most of the preaching I hear and too much that I do attempts to build upon "common human experience." "Are you depressed? Everyone has been depressed at one time or another. Down in the dumps. There is a story of someone who was down in the dumps, in the pit, so to speak. His name was Joseph. He was thrown into a pit. What did he do? That is the theme of my sermon. . . ."

As the feminists have reminded us, "common human experience" is a dubious claim. Too often the assertion of "common human experience" is a political revelation of who is doing the talking, whose experience is made primary. Also, the text's claim is more than the mere expression of allegedly common human experience. The text wants to shape our human experience, to judge it. For instance, depression may be a therapeutic problem for us. We live in an affluent culture that places many unbearable and trivial burdens upon us. Depression may be a positive sign of progress for the Bible. In many prophetic texts, grief is the beginning of the creation of space, a first act of resistance against the status quo. The Bible may have nothing against our depression, may even want to provoke depression. The Bible doesn't just build on human experience. It rearranges our experience and gives us a way of naming our pain rightly.

I was in Mississippi, leading a study of Romans, Romans 6. "Do you not know that all of us who have been baptized into Christ Jesus were baptized into his death? We were buried therefore with him by baptism into death. . . . Our old self was crucified. . . . We have died with Christ" (Romans 6:3, 4, 6, 8, RSV).

Dumb stares from the group of assembled laity. In desperation I asked, "Has anyone here ever had to *die* to be a Christian? I know that we didn't put enough water on you to kill you at your baptism, but did any of you have to die?"

Silence.

Then someone spoke. "When the schools of Jackson integrated, I thought I would die. I knew enough to know that, on that day, when black children went to school with white, it was over for us. Our world was gone. But now my neighbor, and best friend, is black. An old world died but a new world was born."

"OK. Anyone else?"

"I was always afraid to be in the house alone. When my husband went away on overnight business trips, I always went with him, or else took the kids to a friend's house. Then the day my daughter died of leukemia, I have never been afraid to be alone again."

"I'm sorry," I said, "I don't get the connection."

14

"Well, when you've died, what else is there to fear? When you've had to let go of the most precious possession of your life, what else could they do to you that would be worse?"

In *People of the Truth*,[9] Robert Webber and Rodney Clapp called my attention to a delightful story by Garrison Keillor about Sveeggen, a farm boy of twelve, left alone with chores to do in the family barn. He heard the wind begin to howl and looked out the barn door into a fierce blizzard. To his horror, he saw the family home engulfed in flames. Running out the barn door into the blizzard, he became disoriented in the white wilderness. He knew that he was lost in the snow and would die.

Then suddenly he saw the house again. He walked toward the orange glow and warmed himself by the flames. Regaining his bearings, he then "ran straight into the blizzard and ran smack into the side of the barn, where he spent the night, lying next to the cow, Tina, holding his broken nose."

Even into his adult years, Sveeggen never forgot his personal confrontation with death. Like those having been baptized, he responded in gratitude, "How kind is God the Father, we were all lost in sin."

Keillor comments, "Having lost his life he entered a new one with a sweet disposition. He planted trees, raised cattle, married, had seven children, and seldom spoke a harsh word. His nose was never set. He pitched ten tons of hay the day he was married; in their wedding picture, he sits, smiling, his eyes bright beside his ruined beak, a man who took a hard wallop and now everything was easy for him."[10]

Forgive us preachers for presenting the Christian life as a matter of faith development, slow, orderly growth toward the

9. Robert E. Webber and Rodney Clapp, *People of the Truth* (San Francisco: Harper & Row, 1988).

10. Garrison Keillor, *Lake Wobegon Days* (New York: Viking, 1985), pp. 207-8.

goal of psychic wellness. Painless therapy, not major surgery.
Things are messier than that, more costly. We were buried with
him in baptism. Thus all the death we experience, our necessary and unnecessary losses, are given new names in his name.

Forgive us preachers for using argument and syllogism as
our stock-in-trade. Faith's truth is lived. In the light of the
gospel, our lives take on significance we would not have seen
without the gospel. Thus preaching that would be Christian is
always interfacing the gospel story with our story in such a way
that we see that our lives have cosmic significance. In our daily
dying and rising, God is busy making something out of nothing,
life out of death. So the preacher loves to lay the Christian
tradition next to our lives in such a way that we see the story
of Jesus as nothing less than our own.

I am troubled by preaching that is captured by the hermeneutics of translation, as if the gospel can be transposed into some
other idiom that is somehow superior to the gospel. Many
feminist and liberation theologians urge subordination of the
authoritative text to the critical hermeneutics of the experience
of the oppressed. Elizabeth Schüssler Fiorenza writes:

> I would . . . suggest that the revelatory canon for theo-
> logical evaluation of biblical androcentric traditions . . .
> cannot be derived from the Bible itself but can only be
> formulated in and through women's struggle for liberation
> from all patriarchal oppression. . . . The personally and
> politically reflected experience of oppression and liberation
> must become the criterion of appropriateness for biblical
> interpretation and evaluation of biblical authority claims.[11]

In other words, if my experience and therapeutic goals
collide with those engendered by the Bible, too bad for the

---

11. Elizabeth Schüssler Fiorenza, *In Memory of Her: A Feminist Reconstruction of Christian Origins* (New York: Crossroad, 1983), p. 32.

Bible. My experience becomes a judge of Scripture. We have become hermeneutically suspicious of biblical experience and uncritically accepting of our own. We arrogantly relegate the Bible to "androcentric traditions," throwing ourselves back upon ourselves. Such reading continues to assume that it is possible for the Bible to make sense apart from the embodiment of the community (church) which makes it make sense. In the beginning of this section, we quoted David Buttrick's characterization of preaching as having a "double consciousness." The congregation is both those who are being saved by the gospel and those who are in the world. But we do not know the "world" until the gospel describes it. The gospel teaches us to name that world, a world that is both God's creation and God's greatest problem. Without the church, its life together and message, we would have no way of naming the world as both fallen and being saved, nor of naming ourselves, of knowing what aspects of someone's "experience of oppression and liberation" (Fiorenza) are significant. We must not exchange the error of a radically historicized and intellectualized interpretation of Scripture (historical criticism) for a reading that is radically subjectivized. So while Christian preaching struggles for connections, associations between my life and the word of the gospel, it also expects disassociation, gaps, tension between my story and the gospel. Disassociation employs a wide array of homiletical devices — dialectic, paradox, irony, argument, and perhaps most effective of all, humor.

Because we are preaching among the baptized, we preach to those who have been called out from the world in order, by their life together, to witness to the world that God has brought creation out of chaos and has every intention of completing that which was begun.

According to Luke, immediately after his baptism in the Jordan, Jesus returns to his hometown synagogue in

17

Nazareth. The Spirit having descended in baptism, Jesus speaks the word in the Spirit:

> And he stood up to read; and there was given to him the book of the prophet Isaiah. He opened the book and found the place where it was written,
>
> "The Spirit of the Lord is upon me,
> because he has anointed me to preach good news
>   to the poor,
> He has sent me to proclaim release to the captives
> and recovering of sight to the blind,
> to set at liberty those who are oppressed,
> to proclaim the acceptable year of the Lord."
>
> And he closed the book, and gave it back to the attendant, and sat down; and the eyes of all in the synagogue were fixed on him. And he began to say to them, "Today this scripture has been fulfilled in your hearing." And all spoke well of him, and wondered at the gracious words which proceeded out of his mouth; and they said, "Is not this Joseph's son?" And he said to them, "Doubtless you will quote to me this proverb, 'Physician, heal yourself; what we have heard you did at Capernaum, do here also in your own country.'" And he said, "Truly, I say to you, no prophet is acceptable in his own country. But in truth, I tell you, there were many widows in Israel in the days of Elijah, when the heaven was shut up three years and six months, when there came a great famine over all the land; and Elijah was sent to none of them but only to Zarephath, in the land of Sidon, to a woman who was a widow. And there were many lepers in Israel in the time of the prophet Elisha; and none of them was cleansed, but only Naaman the Syrian." When they heard this, all in the synagogue were filled with wrath. And they rose up and put him out of the city, and led him to the brow of

the hill on which their city was built, that they might throw him down headlong. But passing through the midst of them he went away. (Luke 4:16-30, RSV)

I take this as an example of baptismal speaking. All of this occurs in Luke, right after Jesus' baptism. They hand him the scroll, the Scriptures of Israel. They do not ask Jesus, "Tell us how it is for you." They do not ask him to report on his days at college, to share his feelings with them. They hand him the scroll. They ask him to read. Then he interprets, then he preaches. Watch closely as they hand him the scroll because right there, in that action of handing Jesus the scroll, we see a movement that is at the very heart of the faith of Israel.

There may be religions that begin with long walks in the woods, communing with nature, getting close to trees. There may be religions that begin by delving into the recesses of a person's ego, rummaging around in the psyche. Christianity is not one of those religions.

Here is a people who begin with that action of taking up the scroll, being confronted with stories of God, stories that insert themselves into our accustomed ways of doing business and challenge us to change or else be out of step with the way things are now that God has entered human history.

They hand Jesus the scroll. He reads from the prophet Isaiah, speaking of that day when God would again act to set things right, to come for Israel, to lift up the downtrodden and push down the mighty. The Spirit of the Lord is upon him to announce God's advent.

The congregation grows silent as the young preacher reminds them, "Were not there many sick people in Israel during the time of the prophet Elisha? Yes. But Elisha healed none of them. Only Naaman, a Syrian, a Syrian army officer."

And the once adoring congregation becomes an angry mob. As they lead the young preacher out, he says to them,

"I've preached nothing new. It's all in the book! It's all in *your* book!"

A distinctive community is being formed here by this reading and listening. A peculiar community is being criticized here as well. The church was called into being, as if out of nothing, as a people in dialogue with Scripture. Unlike conventional forms of human organization, the church had no ethnic, gender, or national basis for unity. All it had were these stories called Scripture. These Scriptures yielded a person, a personality, Jesus. For this new and distinctive community called the church, Jesus of Nazareth, as the Messiah, became the interpretive framework for all reality, the organizing principle for all of life. And it is so easy to forget how odd, how countercultural and potentially conflictive is such baptismal speaking.

Justo and Catherine Gonzalez have put it this way:

> It is within the community of the baptized that we are preaching. As such, we are, or at least we ought to be, a people with a different vision of reality. As people who are born again through water and the Spirit, we must see all of reality under a different light. . . . What we seek to do through worship is, among other things, to renew and clarify the vision that derives from our new birth. This is the wider context of our preaching. It is not simply the world around us. It is the world seen and judged from the perspective of a people who have been set aside for a mission, born again into a new people. This is not otherworldliness. . . . It is, rather, a matter of accepting and affirming this world as the proper context for our preaching and for our entire Christian lives; but at the same time seeing it under a different light or from a new perspective.[12]

12. Justo and Catherine Gonzales, in *Preaching As a Social Act,* ed. Arthur Van Seters (Nashville: Abingdon, 1988), p. 34.

20

Some time ago, the biblical journal *Interpretation* published an issue devoted to explication of the Decalogue, the Ten Commandments. John Howard Yoder was asked to explicate "Thou shalt not kill."

I can't remember Yoder's exact statements about this commandment, but I can remember his method of interpretation, principally because it was so utterly different from my own.

Thou shalt not kill. God's people are not allowed to destroy what God has lovingly created, said Yoder. This is a simple, straightforward command. Thou shalt not kill. I realized that, through years of scholarship (I went to Yale, you know), I had been conditioned to disregard this text, immediately to rearrange the text rather than my own life. Then Yoder asked, What sort of people would have been necessary to have obeyed such a command? What sort of human community would have been evoked by such divine summons? Of course, it would necessitate a people quite different from many of our contemporary expressions of church. It would be no government, democratic or any other. It would be a people willing to let God reign, a people creative enough to envision social structures and methods of organization different from conventional means of human community. Isolated individuals, private conscience, or majority rule would all be incapable of sustaining people who refused to kill.

Through years of schooling, I had been trained not to take such texts with any real seriousness, certainly with no political seriousness. I had been conditioned to say, almost reflexively. "Thou shalt not kill. Now, under what conditions would it be appropriate to kill? Capital punishment? Just war? Self-defense?"

It had never occurred to me to take the text more seriously than my own objections. It had never occurred to me that the text meant not simply to describe the human condition, but to critique and reorganize that condition. Why had I not taken this text as seriously as Yoder? Because I had been part of an interpretive community (mainline liberal Protestantism) where we were formed into the belief that my individual consciousness was superior to the Bible's call for me to be converted into a new consciousness, that the modern, democratic nation's periodic need for soldiers was superior to the Bible's invitation to be part of a new people who trust the truth which is Christ rather than the sword.

A command not to kill presupposes that a new community will be required to be obedient to a righteous and holy God, a community based upon something more significant than common human experience. The text itself is generated by a specific community, not by general human aspiration. The text, in turn, is capable of generating a community worthy to hear it. That new community is evoked, equipped in baptism. In baptism we are taught to find our strength in God and God's people rather than ourselves. We are prepared for the shock of moral transformation by a cleansing, cold bath. We are born, drowned, adopted, clothed, gifted so that we might be a people worthy of listening to a peculiar account of human life called Scripture.

To begin to preach from the perspective of baptism, assuming that these words are not meant for everyone but only for those who have been or who are to be baptized, is to speak in a new key. It is to listen to Scripture with the expectation that we may well hear the unexpected. It is to preach to a congregation with the assumption that no conventional human gathering will be adequate to hear such words, that a new gathering will be necessitated by such language. Too much of our theology and preaching has acted as if we need new language in order to maintain our old, conventional means of human gatherings. Biblical language has shown, time and again, that it has power, like the sacrament of baptism itself, to evoke that of which it speaks. The Bible is able to create, re-create the people it desires. The sacraments have "the same office as the Word of God," says Calvin, "to offer and set forth Christ to us, and in him the treasures of heavenly grace" (*Institutes,* IV, 14, 17).

We know not whether to speak of such speaking and listening as death or birth.

"The Invitation"

Third Sunday of Easter
Matthew 20:1-15

JESUS said that God's Kingdom is like a man who had a vineyard that needed harvesting. The man goes out into the marketplace and hires some workers, agreeing to pay them one denarius a day. They go to work.

Mid-morning he looks over his vineyard and sees that more workers will be needed if the job is to be done, so he goes back into the marketplace where he encounters some men still standing around whom no one has hired. Even though a third of the day is over, he asks them to go to work for him, telling them that he will pay them what's right.

At noon, when he goes back downtown, he sees some guys hanging out on the street corner, and invites them to come to work in his vineyard, telling them that he will pay them what's right.

At three, he's back downtown where he spies a couple of young men with nothing to do and, even though the sun is beginning to move toward the far west, what the heck? He hires them, promising to pay them what's right.

Finally, at five P.M., he goes back to town one more time. Now, there's almost no one left loitering on the street corner. After all, the day is almost over. But there are two men, leaning up against the wall of the unemployment office. Even though it's only one hour before quitting time, he hires them as well.

So if you're keeping score, by the end of the day we have different groups of workers in the vineyard who have been there for twelve hours, for nine hours, for six, three, and one hour.

Now, they will be paid. If you will recall, a wage was agreed upon only for those who got there first. A denarius. But this peripatetic employer pays those who got there last, first. To everyone's amazement, he pays those who have only worked one hour a denarius. So that means that those who have worked for twelve hours, sweating in the vines all day long, will probably get . . . twelve denarii?

No, they get what they agreed to work for, a denarius.

There are murmurings of injustice. Is this any way to run a business? No, the injustice is only apparent. They agreed to work for a denarius. They have been given a denarius.

Now Matthew, in his editorial introduction to this parable (19:30), suggests that the parable has something to do with Jesus' statement that "many that are first will be last, and the last first" (Mark 10:31).

"Oh," say the disciples, "we get the point. Those Pharisees, who have criticized you for eating and drinking with sinners, think they are first in God's kingdom. But because of their insufferable self-righteousness and smugness, they are really going to end up on the outside and we shall end up on the inside. The first shall be last, and the last shall be first."

"Oh," said the early church, "we get your point, Jesus. Those Jews, who were supposed to be God's Chosen People, the inheritors of your kingdom, they rejected you so now those who were to be first shall be last and we Gentiles, who were supposed to be last, get to be first. We are those who came late to God's kingdom but we get the same reward as those who have been here through all the ages."

25

Well, we can certainly understand those Pharisees, those Jews who murmured and grumbled over God's generosity in Jesus, coming to us, as God did, so late in the day, after they had believed (and suffered, too) down through ages of persecution, misunderstanding, and exile. But, that's tough. Even though we are last, we get the same generous grace that God offered to them so long ago. The first shall be last, the last, first.

God's grace is the same for the last as for the first. The wages are the same for the last as for the first.

But such an interpretation may not get at the true scandal of this little story.

*　　　*　　　*

On the first day of class the professor says, "Now students, I have this complicated, very complicated, math problem, the solution of which shall constitute your grade for the entire semester. I'm giving you this problem here at the beginning of the semester so you all can start work immediately, and I do urge you to begin immediately if you hope to pass the course. I want you all to make A's."

Well, you want to do well. So you get the problem and go to work, first week of the class. You go to the library. There you search for books that may be helpful. You begin calculation.

To your surprise, you note that, even by mid-February, only a few of your fellow classmates have begun work on the problem. Well, that's their business. They will be sorry come May. You have been at work since the second week of January.

The week before exams, you are proudly putting the finishing touches on your paper and the solution to the problem. Some in the class tell you that, if they work hard over the next few days, they may get it finished. There are others who haven't even begun. There is no way for them to be finished no matter what. But, that's their problem.

Then comes the last day of the semester. You proudly bring your work by to hand it in to the professor. To your surprise, all the others also have their work finished. How did they do it? You are about to learn how.

"Professor Smith, thanks for helping me figure this out last week. Why, without your help, I would never have gotten it finished," you overhear one to say.

"Well, here it is, Professor Smith. All done, thanks to your kind assistance yesterday," says another.

"Thanks for coming by the dorm last night to help me," says another.

You are aghast. No wonder they finished their work. While you were hard at work, figuring it out on your own, this professor has been all over the campus spoon-feeding it to everybody in the class, everybody but you, that is.

When you tell Professor Smith what you think of it, she says, "Why do you begrudge my generosity? The goal of the class is to get people to finish the problem. You were able to finish it on your own. Fine. The others needed a little special attention. You get an A. They get an A. What's wrong with that? Am I not doing you right?"

Somehow, it just doesn't feel right. You look at your A. It was what you wanted out of the class. But now that everyone else also has an A, what with Professor Smith's forays into the dorm and everything, it doesn't feel like an A.

Isn't it odd how the professor's graciousness doesn't feel like graciousness?

*   *   *

I don't think we'll get at the true scandal of this story by focusing on Matthew's "the last will be first, and the first last." That acts as if the scandal of the story of the workers

27

in the vineyard is that everybody, despite when each arrived, got a denarius, or as if the scandal of the story of the professor is that everybody, despite when they started on the problem, got an A.

That's not really what gets us about this story. After all, a denarius a day is not all that great a wage to begin with. While nobody knows the precise value of a denarius, we do know that it took about a denarius a day to support a laborer and his family at the level of bare subsistence. A denarius a day is not that generous. It's not as if this employer is throwing around money.

The story has little to say about wages anyway. It is mainly concerned with the comings and goings of the owner of the vineyard. He goes out in the early morning and hires workers for the day and that ought to be it. But to our surprise, barely three hours later, he's back again. And then again at noon. And then again and again. We wonder why that vineyard owner was so bound, bent, and determined to hire everybody off the streets he could lay his hands on. Were his grapes already overripe? Did he know it was going to rain tomorrow and the harvest might be ruined? Did he have a soft spot in his heart for the unemployed?

We don't know. The story doesn't say. All that it says, and with great detail, is that this particular master expended a great deal of gasoline going back and forth from his vineyard to town, picking up anybody off the street who would consent to go work for "what's right."

Well, what's right? For us, justice is a matter of giving people what they are worth. Let's see, you worked longer so you should get more. You stayed in school all the way through your BA, your MA, and your PhD. You get more. You have more IQ so it's only right that you should get more. That's justice for us.

But in the story, justice is determined, not by "what is right" (after all, the owner did pay what he agreed to pay, he just paid it to everyone). In the story, justice is determined by the owner's need for laborers. It isn't the denarius that's so generous, it's the owner's repeated, unrelenting call to come into his vineyard. The generosity is not in what is earned, but in the invitation.

He just wouldn't quit going back and forth into town. He just wouldn't stop calling, wouldn't stop hiring, inviting, seeking, offering.

Here is a kingdom that is not structured on justice, what we deserve, what's fair, what's earned. We may structure our kingdoms that way, or at least we attempt to do so. But that's the way we do business. The way God does business is another matter. Persistent, intrusive invitation, not dispassionate justice, is the way this kingdom is structured. We may think that we'll get what we'll get based upon our good efforts, our attempts to be good and to do good. But the story suggests that we'll get what we'll get on the basis of invitation.

The grace in this story is in the owner's frequent forays into town, not in the denarius. The owner is the one who won't be happy until everyone is at work in the vineyard, the professor who won't sleep well at night until everyone in the class gets an A, the giver of a banquet who won't be happy until everyone moves to the music.

If all we want is justice from God, that's all we'll get. Take your denarius and go, says the master. Big deal.

But, through the master's resourceful, intrusive, never-ceasing mercy, we may hope for more than justice, more than just what's right. We may get the master, constantly, persistently, relentlessly pursuing us and everyone else until the midnight hour, unhappy until everyone is there.

I say to you this is an Easter parable. That's why I'm telling it to you today. It's a story — you perhaps can think of others — about a God who refused to leave us alone, refused to leave things with just what's right, a God who came out and pursued us, sought us, found us, sometimes early, sometimes late. You are here this morning, not because you have been given "what you deserve" (who would want that from God?), but because you have been invited. Some of you came early, some late.

And if you are not here this morning, there is still time. The good news is, he's looking for you. Eleventh-hour workers are as sought by him as those who have been here all day. And, if you have been here since early morning, the bad news in the good news is that the master invites, welcomes everyone, even those whom we have despised, thinking that we deserve more than they. Our worth in this vineyard is determined, not by what's right, justice, but by the invitation, who's called. Our Shepherd has yet other sheep to be invited into this fold. The invitation is based, not on how long or hard we've worked, but on the mercy, the pursuing, never-ending mercy. The good news is, he's out looking for you. And the hope, the Easter, resurrection hope is that this God, who has pursued us so in life, shall not stop pursuing us in death, so that in life, in death, come early, come late, *we are invited*.

2

Preaching as
Baptismal Repentance

EVERY time we stand up to preach, we do so amid an all-encompassing ideology of which we are mostly unaware. We don't notice our condition because most of the metaphors and words we use to describe ourselves come to us from the media of the Empire. A consumeristic economy tells us that our worth derives from what we accumulate, and since we can never accumulate enough, never can be sure we have the newest and most improved model of everything, we are kept in perpetual anxiety. Perpetual anxiety produces exhaustion, and exhaustion produces paralysis. And thus there is never birth.

Max Weber noted that capitalism produces a kind of iron cage in which all the tools given by the system for our liberation from the cage only produce stronger bars. We think that we will break loose through the vigorous assertion of our individuality or our personal creativity, only to find that the system makes even such attributes as individuality another commodity, one that is always in too short a supply to free us.

31

Birth comes only after proposing an alternative, only after the evocation of possibility. The best of our preaching has a kind of playfulness about it when in our speaking we invite the congregation to strip down, dive in, splash about, and see what God might make of us.

We are taught to use the word *repentance* for this experience of Sunday detoxification, rejuvenation, and dislocation, but it's alright if you want to call it birth, refreshment, illumination, washing, death, initiation, *baptism*.

When you join Rotary they give you a handshake and a lapel pin. When you join the church we throw you in the water and half drown you. Ponder that. Whatever signing on with Jesus means, it means that we will not do just as we are, that change is demanded, daily, sometimes painful turning and detoxification that does not come naturally.

The human fetus is created in the waters of the womb. The world was formed from chaos when the Creator pushed back the waters. In Jewish apocalyptic thought, the end of the world was described as a new creation, a new beginning (Isaiah 65:17; 66:22; 1 Enoch 91:16-17). In many apocalyptic thinkers, the first creation has become confused and corrupted and needs replacement by some new act of divine creativity (Zechariah 14:6-8). Zechariah prophesies a return to the living water of Eden (Genesis 2:10) from which Adam and Eve had been expelled (Genesis 3:23-24). Water is the medium for dramatic, creative change, for the restoration of divine intentions.

Like preaching, baptism does what the entire liturgy does. It reenacts the death and resurrection of Christ, making present and real all the promise of the new world gained in that death and resurrection. With bodily gestures, use of material elements, and words, baptism is the initiation of the entire person into the story of Israel and Jesus. It is an enactment or drama of the entire history, from

32

creation to resurrection. . . . We can imagine how long it would take simply to read the biblical story from creation to consummation. Yet baptism, a remarkably compact ceremony, leaves none of the story out. . . . To take a new story is to take a new life.[1]

A Baptism of Repentance

Paul constantly referred to his own turning, his own repentance as a model of what it meant to be called by a crucified God. His theology of salvation reaches a high point in Romans 6:1-11. "Do you not know that all of us who have been baptized into Christ Jesus were baptized into his death?" This is the personal counterpart of his theology of the church in Ephesians 4:5, ". . . one Lord, one faith, one baptism. . . ." The power of the cross of Christ erupts into the world through baptism (1 Corinthians 1:17). Baptism is the power of the cross made actual among those who believe, the most immediate aspect of the gospel, which drives Paul to preach. Here is a way of being saved that is implacably paschal. And yet in Paul, as in most of the other New Testament authors, references to baptism are more allusive than descriptive. These authors assume the existence of baptism rather than report in detail how baptismal practices were carried out. When they refer to baptism, their concern is more with meaning than mode.

All of the Gospels begin with the figure of John the Baptizer, a shadowy, prophetic figure out in the wilderness. John does not preach in Jerusalem, at the center of power as the world judges power. He spreads his message from the wilderness. John's message is simple: Get ready. Repent. To

1. Robert E. Webber and Rodney Clapp, *People of the Truth* (San Francisco: Harper & Row, 1988), p. 74.

those who take comfort from their connectedness to the old order and the old power arrangements — we have Abraham as our father, my family founded this church, I voted Democratic in the last election — John tells them that even they, even the Chosen must get washed. God is able to raise up children even out of the stones in the Jordan River.

Jesus' own baptism by John the Baptist in the Jordan is the prototype of Christian practice. John's emphasis is on prophetic expectations of divine cleansing to be consummated in the work of the promised Messiah. His baptism is one of repentance as preparation for Messianic work. The content of John's baptism is based on costly preaching and witness. He demands conversion of life as a precondition for the new age and promises remission of sins. By submitting to John's baptism of repentance, Jesus established his solidarity with those who were the object of John's preaching.

John's baptism is the prototype of Christian baptism because of what happened when it was applied to Jesus. When Jesus was baptized by John in the Jordan, there was an event that at once consummated John's baptism and rendered it obsolete. There was a divine act, a descending of the heavenly dove that manifested Jesus as the long-awaited Messiah of God. Jesus' own baptism is both in contact with John's baptism and yet some distance from it. In Jesus' baptism, the redemptive act of God is set in motion and we see the peculiar way in which God intends to save in Jesus. Jesus says that he has "A baptism with which I must be baptized" (Mark 10:38; Luke 12:50). Subsequent tradition (Romans 6) would look back on that event and its consequences and realize that Jesus demanded repentance — not simply the cleansing of John the Baptist, but a going down unto death as Jesus did. When, in Acts 2, the Spirit is poured out on those who repent, the two baptisms (the water baptism of John and the Spirit baptism of Jesus) have merged without fusion to become the moment of the church's birth, the central metaphor of its life, and the content of its mission (Matthew 28:18-20).

In Acts 2, on the Day of Pentecost, when a once scoffing crowd is pricked to the heart and asks, "What must we do?" Peter's response is simple. "Repent, believe, be baptized." This is how, according to Acts 2, a Pentecostal God raises up children out of the stones in the river. Peter invites the multitude of "Jews and devout people from every nation under heaven" to come forward for a baptism of repentance "In the name of Jesus Christ for the forgiveness of your sins," with the promise that they would receive "the gift of the Holy Spirit."

The goal of such repentance and Spirit giving is the birth of a new people. All birth is a gift, but no birth, particularly that wrought by the Spirit, is without some pain. When Nicodemus comes to Jesus by night (John 3:1-15), Jesus tells him that he must be born "from above" (John 3:3). The Greek word here is *anothen,* which can mean "from the top down" (as when the veil of the temple is torn "from top to bottom," Matthew 27:51). When Nicodemus misunderstands, thinking that Jesus has asked him to be born a second time ("How can anyone be born after having grown old?" John 3:4), Jesus tells him that to enter God's kingdom, one must be "born of water and Spirit" (3:5).

Even as God's Spirit breathed over the primal waters (Genesis 2:7), so baptismal insufflation creates new lives out of old. In the ancient baptismal rites of the West, this was signified by both breathing upon the candidate for baptism and over the baptismal water. All of this is promise that (to quote Tertullian) "the Spirit of God, who hovered over [the waters] from the beginning, would continue to linger over the waters of the baptized" (*On Baptism,* chaps. III-IV). Birth. Water. Spirit. Wind. These are all baptismal, repentance images, images of what it means to enter God's kingdom.

And the waters can be deep. The fetus develops in the

waters of the womb and, toward the end of our lives, we instinctively revert to the position of a fetus. The womb of baptism is also a tomb of death and rebirth. And the waters can be deep.

Sailing Was Now Dangerous

Here is an ancient account of the rough waters of baptism:

Agrippa said to Festus, "This man could have been set free if he had not appealed to the emperor."

When it was decided that we were to set sail for Italy, they transferred Paul and some other prisoners to a centurion of the Augustan Cohort, named Julius. . . . Since much time had been lost and sailing was now dangerous, because even the Fast had already gone by, Paul advised them saying, "Sirs, I can see that the voyage will be with danger and much heavy loss, not only of the cargo and the ship, but also of our lives." But the centurion paid more attention to the pilot and to the owner of the ship than to what Paul said. . . . When a moderate south wind began to blow, they thought they could achieve their purpose; so they weighed anchor and began to sail past Crete. . . . But soon a violent wind, called the northeaster, rushed down from Crete. Since the ship was caught and could not be turned head-on into the wind, we gave way to it and were driven. . . . We were scarcely able to get the ship under control. . . . We were being pounded by the storm so violently that the next day they began to throw the cargo overboard, and on the third day with their own hands they threw the ship's tackle overboard. When neither sun nor stars appeared for many days, and no small tempest raged, all hope of our being saved was at last abandoned. . . . Just before daybreak, Paul urged all of them to take some food, saying, "Today is the fourteenth day that you have been in suspense and remaining without food, having eaten nothing. Therefore I urge you to take some food, for it will help you survive." . . . After he had said this, he took bread; and giving thanks to God in the presence of all, he broke it and began to eat. Then all of them were encouraged and took food for themselves. (Acts 26:32–27:36)

I have long been fascinated that Luke inserts this strange, stylistically unusual, first person, seafaring novella in the middle of his account of Paul's final days on his way to Rome.[2] Why is it here? I think it is here, so dramatically told, toward the end of Acts and Paul's life to indicate that, as Christians, we are part of a journey, a pilgrimage on a vast, dark sea, where our trust in God, begun in the waters of baptism, does not exempt us from terrifying dangers; in fact, baptism intensifies such dangers. To be a Christian is to be someone always close to death-dealing waters. As Jesus told us, every day we must take up his cross and follow. Or as Luther characterized it, every day we must wake up and volunteer for death, praying as we drag out of bed, Keep putting us to death, Lord Jesus, even as you began in our baptism (*The Small Catechism,* sec. III, IV).

From our earliest days, human imagination has been gripped by stories of sea voyages — the travels of Sinbad the Sailor, Odysseus's legendary exploits on the wine-dark sea, Jonah swallowed by a great fish in his attempt to avoid Nineveh, the disciples crying out to Jesus in a storm on the Sea of Galilee. Is it because of the dark perils the sea represents, the threat of watery oblivion? Or are we attracted to these tales of sea journeys because we know that we

2. See my *Acts* in the series Interpretation: A Commentary for Teaching and Preaching (Atlanta: John Knox, 1988), pp. 182-86.

ourselves are voyagers upon uncharted seas, pilgrims at the mercy of the elements? The sea held terror for people in the ancient world. For the Hebrews, the sea represented that watery chaos which the Creator pushed back when the earth was formed from the void (Genesis 1:6-10). The sea burst forth, by God's anger with humanity, wiping out every living thing from the face of the earth in the days of Noah, the first sailor. For Noah and his family, the sea was not only the source of God's judgment upon human sin but also the place of gracious divine deliverance for God's faithful ones. The flood waters were a time of *metanoia,* of turning around for the human race, as well as a time for God to repent and promise never again to give up on us. The waters that destroyed were also those that purified and delivered. And when at last we are the recipients of a re-created and restored new heaven and new earth, the sea, that great, threatening abyss, shall be no more (Revelation 21:1).

Even today, the sea represents a place of peril, of human vulnerability, the place where would-be sailors are at the mercy of the elements. Only recently I presided at a memorial service for a Duke student who drowned in Costa Rica while volunteering in a project designed to help save the rain forest. The first student to speak at her service said, "I can't figure it out. She spent her whole life loving nature, living in nature, and in the end nature killed her."[3]

Nature, watery, death-dealing nature is as much a threat as a friend. This is the threatening world that Paul penetrates, resists, and endures in this tale of a storm at sea. "We put to sea," says the narrator of this section of Acts (27:2), and Paul's adventure begins.

Knowing that his life is involved in God's mission (27:24),

---

3. For a wonderful account of the sea as image for the postmodern dilemma, see J. D. Crossan, *The Dark Interval: Towards a Theology of Story* (Niles, Ill.: Argus, 1975).

Paul not only has courage but seeks to fill his shipmates with courage as well (27:25). Paul's decisive confidence contrasts with the fear of the soldiers. Their swords give them no defense against the storm. In the ultimate act of confidence, Paul urges his companions to eat. He took bread, blessed it, broke it, and began to eat (27:35). This repetition of the familiar fourfold table action by which the Risen Lord was revealed (Luke 24:30-31) is a source of encouragement for all on board (27:36). What is the response of the church in times of discouragement and fear? Like Paul, the church takes bread, blesses it, breaks it, and begins to eat. "What good will that do?" the world may ask, the world that trusts swords more than eucharistic bread. In this sign of hope in the power and presence of God, this eucharistic witness to our confidence in God's will to give us what we need, the church not only feeds itself but also witnesses to the world. Of course, we are not told that Paul's breaking of bread was what we call the sacrament of the Lord's Supper. Nor are we told whether or not the pagans on board joined with Paul in his blessed food. Yet surely Theophilus's church would make the connection between their Sunday meals together in whatever "storm" they were traveling through and this meal on a dark day at sea. The church is none other than those who speak a word of hope and then break bread in the middle of the storm.

In the storm, the world's legions, its entrepreneurs and beneficiaries, see the storm only as a sign of chaos. We are taught to name such storms as times of dismantlings, as opportunities for rebirth, as occasions for witness (Luke 21:5-33).

Preaching and Conversion

Preaching is a baptismal act when it asserts that *the Christian life is available only to those who submit to dismantling and rebirth, to conversion.* Submission is a dirty word in a culture of democratic individualism. We get the impression, listening to many of our sermons, that Christianity involves holding certain beliefs that are helpful in making sense of our lives as they already are, a technique for greater self-esteem. Faith in Jesus is subservient to our desires for ourselves. Despite our earnest pleas in behalf of good things like community, such preaching only reinforces the assumption that salvation is an individual matter. Community is, like everything else, only a technique for enhancing the lives of individuals. Even when preachers urge their congregations to get out and work for a more just society, the ideal society envisioned is a liberal democratic one whose foundational assumptions about the sovereignty of the individual and the sanctity of individual choice undercut the communal, political character of Christian salvation.

Saving people in liberal democratic societies can be as tough as in oppressive communist ones, perhaps even tougher.

I remember talking with a courageous East German pastor who had suffered much from the communists. I could not hide my admiration for him and his church. He became uneasy with my sympathy and said, "It's tough here. But sometimes that's good for the church. There are more people in church on a Sunday in East Germany than in West Germany, despite there being many more people there than here. The way I see it, our government hates the church, but because our government is incompetent, it can't destroy the church. The West German government says it doesn't care whether they are Christian or not, and has thereby succeeded in destroying the church."

The difficulties of serving God in a democracy are due to many factors, but one of the most subtle and powerful is the democratic presupposition that the consciousness of the "common man" (or woman) is innately valuable regardless of its formation or lack thereof. Through "self-evident" truths and "inalienable rights" (language from *The Declaration of Independence*) people are presumed to be born good rather than in need of conversion.

Of course, we forget that we all had to be "converted" to the language of individualism and rights. It is not as if Christianity requires conversion, explanation, formation and liberal democracy does not. It is not as if liberal democracy's philosophical premise is something that comes naturally while Christianity's premise (that God rules the world, not the world's nations) requires conversion.

The roots of the democratic view of moral goodness lie in Kant. Kant defined the task of ethics as the discovery and explication of universally valid presuppositions shared by anyone. Without God, ethics turned to the discovery of universals. Ethics is the cataloguing of what all of us already know, even though we may not know it until we've been converted by a course in ethics that tells us we all are born with attributes like reason, a desire for justice, brotherhood, rights, freedom, and so forth. Even when a concept appears to be somewhat countercultural — say a concern for the less fortunate in the community — we are assured that, after proper individual reflection, even these concepts will be recognized as innately human and therefore affirmed by all as universally available common sense. The notions of common sense, reason, and universal humanity are arrogant because they are very particular, culturally conditioned ideas masquerading as the "facts of life."

For instance, when the President of Yale University welcomed the Class of 1994 to Yale, he articulated for them what it meant to be part of "liberal learning":

You take up traditions of learning that are as old as Jerusalem and Athens. . . . It is your time now, and your responsibility, to carry forward America's unique historical conviction that the diffusion of knowledge is the foundation of justice and the surest safeguard of liberty. . . . You must take yourselves seriously. . . . For the strength of institutions of liberal education lies in a fundamental prin-

41

ciple of restraint: Yale College respects the autonomy of every individual here. . . . The traditions and values of liberal education call upon each of you to accept the responsibility of defining for yourself the aims of learning. . . . The faculty can guide you along the paths of the great traditions of learning. . . . But we cannot supply you with a philosophy of education any more than we can supply you with a philosophy of life. This must come from your own active learning, sparked by your own imagination. . . . Yale expects you to take yourself seriously.[4]

I can think of no more conformist, establishmentarian message in a liberal society than the Yale president's call to his freshmen to "take themselves seriously." How does he think they got into Yale? He even tells them that Yale has nothing to teach them that they basically don't already know. This may come as a shock, considering the high tuition of places like Yale and Duke. They are able to do their own education at a great cafeteria called the university because, according to President Schmidt, they already have, just as they are, all they need in order to know what is right, true, and good. Yale only encourages them to "be yourselves," "to make up your own minds," which is what they have been doing before they came to Yale.

One of the characteristics of a society of normlessness is that it exalts social disintegration as normality and requires a rigid conformity to its ideal of life without family, norms, tradition, stories, or community. I have noted, here at my university, that the people whose primary value is "tolerance" (an Enlightenment invention for people who have absolutely no means of living together other than by keeping their distance from one another) are rather brutally intolerant of

4. President Benno Schmidt, "The Freshman Address," *Yale* (Oct. 1990), pp. 55-56.

those who assert norms. These heretics from the dominant view are quickly labeled "fanatics," "narrow-minded," or "conformist" by those who, like President Schmidt, seem unaware of what a socially conformist gospel they preach.

Contrary to President Schmidt's claim that such knowledge is "as old as Jerusalem," Jews and Christians have known another way to truth, a way running through the community and its life with its Scriptures. In baptism, the Christian faith doubts that we already have minds worth making up. Minds worth having come at the end of a long process of submission to the authority of a community and its texts and the disciplined, daily effort to live out the implications of those texts as a community evoked by the texts. While President Schmidt declares that he and the Yale faculty have no "philosophy of life" to share with the freshmen, any smart Yalie can clearly detect a quite well-developed (and aggressively asserted) philosophy of life behind the president's remarks. It is a philosophy that begins with the presuppositions that the individual is God and that morality is merely the result of the "diffusion of knowledge." In our liberal democratic society we have been taught to regard as unduly authoritarian any account of the moral life that acts as if we become good on the basis of any resources outside ourselves and our choices. Ironically, this has left us susceptible to the worst authoritarian tyranny of all, the self. As Robert Bellah and his colleagues told us in *Habits of the Heart,* "Separated from family, religion, and calling as sources of authority, duty, and moral example, the self first seeks to work out its own form of action by autonomously pursuing happiness and satisfying its wants."[5] Christianity rejects this subjectivization of truth, which conjures up purely private worlds that exist indepen-

5. Robert N. Bellah et al., *Habits of the Heart: Individualism and Commitment in American Life* (Berkeley: University of California Press, 1985), p. 79.

dent of public life. We know of no person, no individual who is not socially shaped. So the question is not, "Will we be socially conditioned?" The question is, "Will the society shaping us be true or false?"

In the popular movie *Dead Poets Society,* we meet a group of privileged, conventional young men who are taught by a courageous young teacher. The teacher urges these conformist, parentally dominated prep schoolers to "think for yourselves." They are to be suspicious of both their textbooks and their parents. Their young, unconventional teacher, like President Schmidt, urges them to think for themselves. Is their teacher pushing an unconventional or a conventional message? As we have said, the call to "think for yourself" message merely encourages rather than defeats conformity to the established ideals of our society.

One of my friends noted that, by the end of the movie, the boys who are members of the Dead Poets Society really are individuals, interesting young men who are now, for the first time in their lives, thinking for themselves, taking hold of their lives. They have become individuals, not by being urged to stand alone, act autonomously, behave independently — the myth of our society. *They are individuals because they are a group.* Their membership in the Dead Poets Society has given them the resources they needed for true individuality. The group enabled them to stand against their ambitious and domineering parents, the inhuman school authorities, and the other social forces that were smothering them. The movie is thus a testimonial, but not to the need for independence, autonomy, and people who can "think for themselves." The movie is a tribute to the power of socialization and the necessity of a truthful, loving group for the nurturing of true individuality. In our better moments, the church has always known this. Without a group of friends to sustain us, we are apt to be victims of the powerful pressures of the nation. We are indeed apt to go out and kill

44

others who will not adhere to our universals, who will not be part of "the new world order."

Against Kant's democratic view of morality, Christianity offers an unabashedly "elitist" account of morality, an account much more like that of Aristotle's moral aristocrat than Kant's common man.

Moral good is not available to anyone, regardless of his or her point of view. In order to be moral, a person must be made into a particular kind of person if that person is to know what is good. Skills and habits like honesty, humility, courage, self-knowledge do not come easily nor do they come naturally. Random accumulation from "the diffusion of knowledge" has little to do with it. In short, we must be born again, and again. We must be adopted.

Kant acted as if the mind required for morality is immediately adequate to the task without training, without submission to authority. Christian baptism denies this. It names prebaptismal preaching as an invitation to be washed, reborn, changed via adoption and postbaptismal preaching as part of a lifelong process of submission, repentance, conversion, and formation.

In this strange, eschatological community, knowledge comes through conversion, by letting go, by submitting to the example of the saints, by being initiated into a community whereby we are positioned to receive the first true knowledge we ever had.

Having had ways of construing reality drowned in baptism, the baptized will probably read the signs of the times as signs of dismantling and delegitimating. Repentance. Detoxification. Having been forced to let go in baptism, having had our fingers wrenched loose from that which we formerly grasped, we begin to read what others see as mere social disintegration as signs of dismantling, as the loss of a known world so that something can be born.

Paul, in describing what happened to him on the Damascus road, knew not whether to describe it as birth or death. Baptism feels like both. The womb is first a tomb.

Baptismal preaching is not a time to report on change that has happened somewhere else, as though the sermon were a history lecture or a journalistic report on something that happened to someone else. The sermon provokes a collision, a bringing back into speech of what happened to us in baptism, and happens whenever God collides with the world. "Emmanuel" means that each of us, in our own faith journey, becomes a microcosm, recapitulating in our own lives what is happening in all creation: relinquishment, letting go, drowning so that there might be change, renewal, transformation, newness, birth.

Baptism is *promise* and *summons,* promise to the unbaptized and mandate to the baptized. What is promised, and thereby evoked, is a new world. Without a promise, we have no way to break free of the status quo. Our repentance is puny because our promising is puny. Something big must embrace us before we can let go of that to which we so tightly cling. Today's church practices no more than liberal "social responsibility," helping George keep a lid on things, when we should be preaching radical social possibility.

> The preaching task, sermon by sermon, text by text, is to enable the listening congregation, one at a time and all together, to relinquish the world dying before our eyes, and to embrace the new world of God's faithfulness that is . . . crowding in on us, but only glimpsed most days.[6]

The preacher brings to speech the awesome dismantling that the world can only describe as economic, political, social problems to be solved. Generalization will not do in baptismal preaching. The tone has been set in water and

6. Walter Brueggemann, "Some Missing Prerequisites," pp. 26-27.

46

the word for speech that must be specific, here, in this time and place, concrete, a matter of taste and touch, the everydayness of the bath, the ordinariness of water, the terror of the open sea. Preaching will want to name the congregation's specific, ordinary, everyday living as part of a cosmic drama that God is writing. We are on a journey. We are at sea. Baptismal preaching will not leave us just as we are. Little wonder then that old Tertullian, when asked about the advisability of delaying baptism for infants, said that delayed baptism is preferable to rashly administered baptism, because "If any understand the weighty import of baptism, they will fear its reception more than its delay" (*On Baptism,* chap. XVIII).

As One with Authority

In 1835, August Tholuck wrote one of the nineteenth century's most popular books on preaching. In Tholuck's foreword to his second collection of *Sermons,* he spoke "A Word Concerning Preaching for the Cultured People of Our Day."[7] After noting how, in one German town after another, modern, educated people had deserted the churches, Tholuck asked, "What can be done to bring the educated classes back again to take part in our worship services? . . . We must offer the hand to the 'Cultured Despisers of Religion' [Schleiermacher] . . . in a time when Shakespeare is a stronger authority for many than is Paul and Goethe a stronger influence for many than the Epistle to the Romans. . . ." To accomplish this, according to Tholuck, the preacher must speak, "not merely as a preacher to us, but as a human being. . . . It is not enough that one speaks the truth, it is essential *how* one

---

7. In *Werke,* vol. 2, *Sermons I* (Gotha, 1863), p. viii.

speaks, . . . how the preacher bears the hopes, pains, and joys of the congregation so that they might hear."

Looking back more than a century, we have difficulty imagining just how radical was Tholuck's proposal. He was proposing that the action of the sermon shift from the pulpit to the congregation, from the orthodoxy of the speaker to the requirements of the congregation. If the congregation had now made Shakespeare more authoritative than Paul, if the congregation now wanted feeling more than theology, then preachers must adjust or else be stuck with empty pews. The humanity of the preacher had moved center stage as the content of preaching and the needs of the congregation as preaching's ultimate standard.

Surely the most influential book on preaching in our time has been Fred Craddock's *As One without Authority*.[8] That book introduced American preachers to what Craddock calls "the inductive method of preaching." He says that "inductive movement in preaching corresponds to the way people ordinarily experience reality and to the way life's problem-solving activity goes on naturally and casually. . . . This method respects rather than insults the hearer and . . . leaves the freedom and hence the obligation to respond" (p. 66).[9]

A central category for the inductive preacher, says Craddock, is freedom. "Every man has the right to be fully human and this means the right to choose for himself" (p. 17). Freedom is not freedom to obey God or the result of a well-formed character. Freedom is the individual's "room to choose" (pp. 146, 157).

Freedom is not freedom to choose or to reject Christ, or

8. Fred B. Craddock, *As One without Authority: Essays on Inductive Preaching* (Enid, Okla.: Phillips University Press, 1971).

9. I am indebted to Chuck Campbell's unpublished paper "What Do Joseph Fletcher and Fred Craddock Have in Common?" (Duke University, 1989) for helping me to describe the problems within *As One without Authority*.

the freedom of all the baptized to wrestle together over the implications of the gospel. Freedom, in *As One without Authority,* is freedom of the individual, apart from Scripture or community, to draw his or her own democratic conclusions. This is an example of what Alasdair MacIntyre in *After Virtue* calls "emotivism," the primary stance of modern people that renders all other stances subordinate to the sovereign individual.

Note that the whole stress here is on *method* rather than *message.* Says Craddock, "the method is the message. So it is with all preaching: *how* one preaches is to a large extent *what* one preaches" (p. 52). What one preaches, it seems, is the individual's freedom of choice in the moment. The inductive method "calls for incompleteness, a lack of exhaustiveness in the sermon. It requires of the preacher that he resist the temptation to tyranny of ideas rather than democratic sharing" (p. 64). Nothing is said here about the tyranny of sin, the tyranny of the cultural status quo, the tyranny of the congregation, economic factors, social class, or all the other masters that (have we not learned in a century of social analysis?) make the notion of individual "freedom of choice" extremely difficult to sustain. Craddock assails "second hand Calvinism that has darkened the air with gloomy reminders that 'we are only human'" (p. 126). In short, we are capable of listening so well and so freely because we no longer sin.

In a way, Craddock's title says it all: *As One without Authority.* "No longer can the preacher presuppose the general recognition of his authority as a clergyman, or the authority of his institution, or the authority of Scripture" (pp. 14-15). Craddock's evidence for why this is so is exclusively cultural rather than theological. "The inductive method is fundamental to the American way of life" (p. 58).

As One without Authority was the culmination of the project begun long ago in the homiletical work of Tholuck. The beginning and end of preaching is in the cultural situation of its recipients. Style can be taken much more seriously than substance (not *what* is said but *how*) because the preacher assumes that the listeners already have the gospel and merely await the preacher to evoke it within them through skillful stylistic appeal. Tholuck's preaching sought merely to evoke the gospel in nineteenth-century Germany rather than to convert nineteenth-century Germany.

American culture now determines the boundaries of the church's speech. Indeed, there seems to be no interest here in the power of language to shape culture — all of the traffic is moving in the other direction. ". . . Our generation is walking the first mile of primary data, the seen and the heard, and out of this raw material sermons are built" (p. 73). The preacher is merely the receiver of the "primary data" of our situation who reflects this in the sermon (p. 90). Craddock's inductive preacher seems so sure that we know what is happening out there and at the same time knows so little about what is the gospel. The individual listener is king. Yet any description of our situation is partly dependent upon the way in which we describe that situation, what our language enables us to see and to say. The world is not self-interpreting. Nor was it the gospel that taught us to describe our dilemma as a limitation of individual freedom.

Preachers must be more than merely receptive to and reflective of the world around them. As Christians we know of no way other than the gospel-evoked community (church) that enables us to receive the world truthfully. The character of the congregation and preacher, how they have each been formed or malformed as listeners, makes a big difference in our ability to preach and to hear the Word. Otherwise, all we've got in "inductive preaching" is an individual preacher reflecting his or her experiences in an open-ended, detached way to a group of individuals who are invited to draw their own conclusions based upon their own experiences.

It should be noted that *As One without Authority* was one of Craddock's earliest books. It was a *tour de force,* an overstated thesis, something all good preachers (and Craddock is a very good one indeed) occasionally advance. His later works definitely put more emphasis on the place of Scripture in our preaching. In his *Preaching* he makes a helpful distinction between a "congregation" and an "audience," similar to the distinction I made earlier about the peculiarity of those who gather under the aegis of baptism.[10] My favorite Craddock book is his first, *The Pre-Existence of Christ in the New Testament,* where he demonstrates a marvelous marriage of New Testament scholarship with deep pastoral concern.[11]

A quite different notion of authority is found in the baptismal mandate at the close of Matthew's Gospel:

> All authority in heaven and on earth has been given to me. Go therefore and make disciples of all nations, baptizing them in the name of the Father and of the Son and of the Holy Spirit, teaching them to observe all that I have commanded you; and lo, I am with you always, to the close of the age. (Matthew 28:18-20)

If discipleship came naturally, if we were capable of hearing the Word as we are, then we would not need to *make* disciples by baptizing and teaching, we would not need the promise "lo, I am with you" to make the gospel credible.

One of the most arrogant imperialisms of modernity and the Enlightenment is its refusal to acknowledge the world in which we live as a social contrivance. Kant (et alia) speak of matters like "justice," "truth," and "reason" as if they were

10. Fred B. Craddock, *Preaching* (Nashville: Abingdon, 1985), chap. 5.
11. Fred B. Craddock, *The Pre-Existence of Christ in the New Testament* (Nashville: Abingdon, n.d.).

givens. The "individual" to whom we modern preachers so want to speak is not a universal given. The individual is a relatively modern construct of a relatively small number of industrialized societies that have devised constitutions in an attempt to hold together people who have absolutely nothing in common, not even God.

The Enlightenment's first attack was aimed at religious orthodoxy and the societies it spawned. It assaulted the mystification of religion that pretended that the present (the eighteenth-century) world was a social given. At the same time, the Enlightenment was blind to the world that its own scientific positivism was busy creating with its presumptions of reason, objectivity, neutrality, Western superiority, colonialism, and racism. It behaved as if it were possible to have a world constructed without story and without community, which, in an ironic sense, eventually became its own story and produced its own community — a community of people whose story is the claim that they are individuals who have not been formed by a story.

The epistemological issue leads to the evangelical question. Matthew 28:20 is still valid only for a church convinced that there is no way for humanity to know the nature and will of God other than through this Jew from Nazareth. Why would we go to the trouble to bother the rest of the world with our evangelistic testimony? Only out of our conviction that there is no way to know God and to obey God other than by knowing and obeying Jesus. This is not Christian arrogance. It is rather the humble witness that we would not have known either ourselves or the world had we not been known by this Jewish carpenter from Nazareth. It is our conviction that humanity cannot know God through the affirmation of certain lofty human ideals, nor through the embrace of certain programs for human betterment, nor by the imperialistic pseudo-baptism of generally good people as "anonymous Christians" (Karl Rahner). It is only by the shock, inconvenience, and utterly gifted bath of baptism that we can know God.

I have spent all of this time on Craddock's *As One without Authority* as an example of how mainline American Protestantism keeps acting as if the contemporary cultural situation, described through the conventional language of that culture, is a fixed entity to which the gospel must be made relevant. Baptism suggests that our homiletical effort is better spent helping contemporary culture (as it gathers in your church and mine on Sunday) to be relevant to the gospel. Without that act of prophetic resistance and reformation, all our vaunted talk of "freedom" is but the rattling of the chains binding us to the authoritarianism of a liberal, democratic culture, a culture that, whether it intended to do so or not, destroys human community by fragmenting us into a herd of isolated units, each detached from tradition, community, history, and one another, all the while telling us that we are free. Ironically, in such a condition, detached from sources of true meaning, we have not gained our individuality but have lost it, for true individualism comes only for someone who knows and can name who she is. Of course, the democratic Empire now knows what the monarchs of old did not: detached, rootless, historyless individuals are more easily managed than people in groups, people who have names, stories, histories, and a home.

A Sense of Largeness

The individual and his or her present consciousness is too small a canvas on which to confine Christian preaching. Only the gospel, as articulated in the church's canon, offers us and our congregations the largeness we lack. When asked why baptism was necessary for salvation, Tertullian admitted that there was much to be said for "bare faith." "But now that faith has been enlarged . . . there has been an amplification added by means of the sealing act of baptism" (*On Baptism,* chap. XIII). Baptism signifies the "enlargement" of faith, the "amplification" of our lives offered by the death and resurrection of Jesus.

Walter Brueggemann reminds us, "Where the sense of largeness is lacking, where we do not understand the crisis of great loss or the alternative of great newness, sermons are twittered away in good advice, happy reassurances, or harsh intimidation."[12]

A few years ago, sitting in the pew, I noted our almost studied efforts to trivialize baptism. Here is power, in water and the word. But what we have up in the chancel is triviality, an affair of cooing babies, grinning parents, droplets from rosebuds, rosey-faced preachers pecking the little darling on the cheek rather than slapping the defiant pagan on the rear. Of course we trivialize preaching too, what with our children's sermons — little moralistic object lessons, sermonettes by preacherettes for Christianettes. It's curious the things we do to children.

Such studied trivializing may be testimony, not to the silliness of baptism and preaching, but to their power. Give the preacher credit, will you? Amid the rosebuds and lace, the brown bags and stories from *Birdlife in Wington,* the preacher knows: there is power here, awesome power to dismantle and to reconstruct, to drown and to give birth. The priest is not only the one who brings us to God but also the one who protects us from God. We trivialize only that which we fear we can't handle, especially God. None of us takes naturally to water.

A child psychotherapist in my congregation remarked that her only objection to children's sermons was that they never dealt with any of the concerns of children. When I asked

12. Brueggemann, p. 27.

"Such as?" she said, "Concerns like death, abandonment, fear of adults, adult injustice, violence."

Ironically, the Bible has the courage to discuss such concerns. Why can't we speak to children with as much depth and complexity as the Bible uses? With what sort of honesty would we have to speak of our family life if we spoke with the words of the Bible rather than with the language of sentimentality and trivialization? The question is important because honest speaking is prelude to change. John the Baptist's "You brood of vipers, who told you to escape the wrath to come?" was the necessary, though painful, prelude to hydrotherapeutic repentance. How do people change? Not by sermons that give advice or urge people to be good, not by moralistic carping and scolding. Only when our imaginations are transformed are we transformed by the "renewing of our mind" as Paul might put it; only when there is a shift in the paradigmatic images by which we construe the world. So when Erich Fromm pondered the story of the sailor, Jonah, and his struggles with the sea and its "great fish," he noted that the story was quite "logical," but "it is a logic of a different kind."[13] The same could be said of most Christian communication, including Christian preaching. Apprehending the world through narrative and symbol is every bit as "logical" as attempts to grasp the world through verbal abstraction. Narrative and symbol, however, may at least claim for themselves a complexity and profundity not found in abstractness. So when change is the preacher's goal, the preacher does well to forsake the sermon's "points" and stick with illustration and story.

Says Brueggemann, "The aim of evangelical preaching is indeed transformation. What is lacking among us is attention to the ways in which transformation happens and the kinds

13. Erich Fromm, *The Forgotten Language* (New York: Holt, Rinehart and Winston, 1951), p. 92.

of wondrous, miraculous speech that permit, authorize, and energize such change. We preachers might well ask of our own experience: Who changed us? How do we change?"[14]

Too much pulpit speech is didactic, moralistic, abstract, reinforcing what we always already thought or else driving us into defensiveness arising out of our inability to conceive of a world other than that which is already thought. There is no other way that people change other than by:

1. *Being adopted by a new family,* which renders previous attachments obsolete.
2. *Being embraced by a vision,* which enables them to let go of present arrangements.
3. *Confessing real grief* that the old is passing away and dying.
4. *Stripping off* those social, cultural, linguistic garments that were previously considered nonnegotiable.
5. *Reverting to some previous innocence* that enables a playful, not overly serious or postured encounter with the world.

In short, transformation is occasioned by something like baptism. Every sermon that would be evangelically transforming does not have to mention baptism, but it must be somehow baptismally formed in order to transform.

Baptism reminds us that gospel is more than an idea. The gospel is a political matter, discipleship. The gospel call is an invitation to a way of living, a matter of style. Preachers are sometimes criticized for a preoccupation with style, with working as much on their medium as their message. In most seminary homiletics classes, we don't care *how* you say something as long as *what* you say is merely correct. But preachers worth their salt know: in baptism or in preaching,

14. Brueggemann, p. 29.

the medium is often the message (thank you, Fred Craddock). We get our ideas right and then ruin them with the
way we say it. We get our baptismal theology right and
then ruin it with the way we do it. Is discipleship a matter
of thinking the right things or a matter of getting the right
moves, internalizing the style of discipleship? Our puny,
miserly, fastidious way of baptism produces puny little
disciples.

Proclamation of the gospel always precedes baptism.
Preaching is the necessary precedent for baptism. The only
exception to this is Paul, who receives not a mediated
proclamation of the gospel but direct revelation from the
Christ himself (Acts 9:1-19). Yet even Paul must undergo
baptism at the hands of Ananias.

The *first* step in the classic initiation process is *proclamation of the gospel.* Calvin says, "the sacrament requires
preaching to beget faith" (*Institutes,* IV, 14, 4).

Second, the normal response of those who hear the gospel
proclaimed is expected to be *conversion* to faith in the exalted
Lord.

The *third* step in the initiation process, the gospel having
been proclaimed and believed, usually results in the *water
bath* itself. A *variety of events* follow water baptism, and these
can be seen as a *fourth* aspect of the initiatory process. The
clearest biblical record of these is in Acts 2:42: "And they
devoted themselves [after baptism] to the apostles' teaching
[didache] and fellowship *[koinonia],* to the breaking of bread
[klasei tou artou] and the prayers *[proseuchais].*" In other
words, the result of the apostolic proclamation, conversion,
and baptism in water and spirit was life in the church, full
participation in the church, a whole new way of life among
Christ and his holy ones.

When New Testament texts refer to "baptism" they mean
something ritually larger and increasingly more sophisticated
and complex than the water bath alone. To be baptized in

water is to be baptized in the Spirit and to take up life among those people whom the Spirit has evoked (Acts 2).

To receive the Spirit through Christ is likened to a *birth bath* in John 3:3-5 and Titus 3:5-7; to a *funeral bath* and burial in Romans 6:1-11; and to a bride's *nuptial bath* in Ephesians 5:26. These baths were consummated in anointing and arraying the body in clean, or new, clothing (Galatians 3:27) as a final stage of the bath itself. Life in this new community is so new and different that conventional social analogies are scarcely adequate to describe it (Galatians 3:28; 1 Corinthians 13:12; Colossians 3:11). Only reference to the most primal human experience — birth, marriage, death and dying — will do.

How can the church best symbolize the fact that the newly baptized convert has now left the powerful cultural context of his or her former life and entered into a new life with new surroundings? The newly baptized are not left to shift for themselves, but are received in full communion with the church by a series of hospitable acts — clothing, public prayer, chrismations, hand-layings, kisses of peace, and admission to the eucharist. A radical break must be accompanied by radical inclusion.

In *The Apostolic Tradition* (c. A.D. 200), Hippolytus specifies,

> When they are chosen who are set apart to receive baptism let their life be examined whether they lived piously as catechumens, whether they honored the widows, whether they visited the sick, whether they have fulfilled every good work. If those who bring them there witness to them that they have done thus, then let them hear the gospel. Moreover, from the day they are chosen, let a hand be laid upon them and let them be exorcised daily.[15]

15. Quoted in Aidan Kavanagh, *The Shape of Baptism: The Rite of Christian Initiation* (New York: Pueblo, 1978), p. 58.

In the baptismal service Hippolytus describes, the elect stripped, loosening their hair and removing all jewelry, lest anyone "go down to the water having any alien object with them." On coming out of the font the neophyte, or *infans,* is signed on the crown of the head. Then they are solemnly robed with stole, chasuble, and given ten coins.

Exorcism played an important part in these rituals, detoxification from the dominant culture. Candidates were led to declare, "I renounce you, Satan, and all your ceremonies and all your works," to which the church promised, "Let every demon depart from you."

My chief point in recounting these ancient rituals is this: How well they knew. One is formed in the gospel, not only by learning, but also by worship, by the every Sunday bending of the life to God, by learning to fall back and let go, by adoption into a new family.

I agreed with Richard Jensen when he noted some time ago,

> If baptism is richly interpreted at a time and place and is a decisive event in the lives of those who undergo it, this both reveals and promotes a richly contoured believing community. If baptism as interpreted at a time and place is puny or speaks inappropriately to the gospel, it is most likely the actuality and self-conception of the church that are antecedently puny or remote from the gospel. And when we perceive such sickness, reshaping of baptism must be and often has been a chief means to reform the church.[16]

No one can review the ancient rites of baptism, as reported by observers like Hippolytus, without being impressed by

16. Robert W. Jensen, *Visible Words: The Interpretation and Practice of Christian Sacraments* (Philadelphia: Fortress, 1978), p. 151.

the expectation of the early church for radical change. These rites of baptism expected a decisive ending of the old life, transformation through the process of initiation, and the beginning of new life. Through instruction, dramatic rite, exorcism, and careful, communal examination, these ancient congregations prepared candidates for the shock of ethical transformation brought about by freeing a person from the grip of the old pagan gods.

Obviously, a great deal happened in the church between 200 and about A.D. 500. The church achieved a *modus vivendi* with the establishment, integrating some of the ceremonies of Caesar into its own rites. Infant baptism became the sign of the disintegration of our rites as well as our self-respect. Infant baptism led, almost inevitably, to a reduction of rite so that the visible word of washing virtually disappeared from the ritual. Sprinkling virtually silenced the visible word of the bath. The physical inconvenience of the bath signified so well the renunciation and risk involved in discipleship. The politics of baptism is a politics of renunciation, and our rites must be strong enough to signify the cost.

Talk of baptism as act of repentance and renunciation, therefore, raises questions about the practice of infant baptism. How can the practice of infant baptism bear such weight?

Whenever it occurs in a person's life, baptism is the paradigm of how faith in Jesus Christ is lived. While some feel that there is no way to rehabilitate infant baptism to make it all that it should be for today's church, I believe that it is not so much infant baptism that debilitates the church as indiscriminate baptism. We must not baptize persons, infants or adults, who do not show a willingness (or a potential willingness) to submit to change. Instruction of candidates for baptism (or, in the case of infants, their parents and sponsors) is essential. Infant baptism is a legitimate pastoral accommodation to the norm of baptism *if* the church is confident that it is able to be the agent of baptismal regeneration in this person's life. If not, then baptism must be postponed until such time as the church feels more confident in its ability to baptize. Such converting work can take place in the infant children of Christian parents or sponsors. However, when the church indiscriminately baptizes infants, regardless of adult and church commitment or lack thereof, then the church is debilitated.

Our objection to so-called believer's baptism should not be that it is not infant baptism but rather that it is defended in the wrong way. Those who baptize only adults sometimes say that they wait to baptize until a person "knows what it means." This rationale owes more to the rationalism of the Enlightenment than to anything biblical. Who "knows what it means"? Baptism "means" not what we as individuals understand by our thinking, decisions, and feelings. Baptism "means" church. It is the church, not the individual recipient, who provides the rationale, the meaning of baptism. The church's way of knowing is inherently communal, political, corporate, a matter not so much of individual decision as of ecclesial discipline. Images of adoption ought to replace images of decision in the way we talk about baptism.

The question is not, "What is the best age for a person's baptism?" The question is, "How can the church best make disciples?" It is the church that bears Christ's mandate to baptize, to make disciples (Matthew 28:19-20).

Basil of Cappadocia's (c. 330-379) *Concerning Baptism* was written by someone whose family had been Christians for generations. Basil's church baptized children of Christian parents as soon as they could answer for themselves. Rather surprising, therefore, is Basil's frequent reference in *Concerning Baptism* to the story of the rich young ruler (Luke 18:18-30). Basil said that, to be baptized, one must first obey the commandments. Then, to be a disciple, one must sell everything one has and follow (Luke 14:33). Basil's words were not directed toward monastics but to all made *christoi* in baptism. The rich young ruler who could not strip down, let go, turn away from the things of the world, and turn to Christ represents, for Basil, the tragedy of the gift of baptism refused.

Note that Luke tells the episode of the rich young ruler immediately following Jesus' statement that none of us can enter the kingdom of God except as a child (18:15-17). So in one sense, all baptism is infant baptism in that none of us can enter this kingdom except with empty hands, small, vulnerable. The rich young ruler turned away from Jesus because he could not let go, become small and vulnerable like a child.

In the Middle Ages, the church lost sight of its own baptismal vision. The rich young ruler became a story only for monks and nuns. The shock of the new, the decisiveness of the turning toward childhood signified in baptism and exemplified in the story of the rich young ruler, was reduced to a rite for babies, welcoming them to the protectorate of a Christian prince.

Our changed cultural situation makes a difference in how we baptize and how we preach. Medieval initiation rites, which have influenced many of our infant baptism practices, were directed not so much at conversion of those outside of the faith as conversion of those within the church to lives of greater individual piety and more intense devotion. Now, images of conversion, communally derived and sustained conversion, must replace those of nurture.

One of the worst defenses of infant baptism is that which speaks of infant baptism as a sign of God's indiscriminate, utterly gratuitous graciousness. The use of baptism in theological apologetics as a sign of God's complete gratuity in the giving of himself must not serve as the basis for a policy of indiscriminate baptism. Such a policy is simply at odds with the New Testament and the church's traditional doctrine of justification by faith in Christ dead and risen. Baptism always involves discernment and discrimination. This is demanded by a gospel that perceives life in Christ as the result of an individual's having willingly entered fully into his passion and death. The church is not the Rotary Club. Being a Christian is not synonymous with being a good human being. If we continue to baptize infants, more time must be spent in discerning intentions — parental intentions and the church's intentions. Are we really prepared to convert people or not? Is the church now structured for such awesome engagement with the growing Christian? The genesis of the church is conversion, conversion in its most ecclesial rather than purely individualistic dimensions. In baptism, as in the Christian faith, we have the sensation of being forced by the community of faith into deep waters, into a lifestyle that does not come naturally, into submission to a project greater than our own lives.

Infant baptism can be a reminder that conversion, and the repentance it entails, is not usually (*contra* much of American evangelicalism) a momentary, instantaneous phenomenon. Baptism, whenever it occurs, sets in motion a lifetime of turning and detoxification. As Luther said, every day of our lives we must wake up and volunteer for death, praying to God to finish in us that which was begun in our baptism.

So when questioned about his recent "conversion" to Roman Catholicism, Richard John Neuhaus replied, "It is not quite accurate to say that I 'converted' to Roman Catholicism. I was converted at three weeks of age when I was baptized. Every day is a day of baptismal conversion, of dying and rising again with Christ, of taking new steps toward becoming more fully what, by the grace of God, we most truly are."[17]

Or as the Westminister Confession puts it, "The efficacy

17. Richard John Neuhaus, "The Future of the Reformation," unpublished address, November 3, 1991, pp. 1-2.

of baptism is not tied to that moment of time wherein it is administered; yet, not withstanding, by the right use of this ordinance the grace promised is not only offered, but really exhibited and conferred by the Holy Ghost . . . in his appointed time" (chap. XXVIII, sec. vi).

For baptism to be the visible word of Spirit induced, the communally encouraged repentance it is meant to be, we must begin, not with words, but with actions. Verbal exhortation and explanation is not enough. In baptism, as in most matters related to the Christian faith, no amount of verbiage can compensate for a lack of action. Baptism without conscientious preparation and celebration is not made right simply by more explanation. In the sacraments, it is futile verbally to impose meaning on an action too attenuated to speak for itself.

In a culture in which people are constantly bombarded with the verbiage of advertising, and where people try to overcome their numbness through the ersatz experience of drugs and alcohol, the church can be thankful that it has been given the gift of more than words. Through the celebration of baptism, we are given access to a radical experience and engagement.

The church awaits more robust celebration of baptism, even as it awaits more robust pulpit speech. When baptism is a bit scary, incomprehensible, dark, primordial, risky, then we have achieved truth in advertising, and discipleship will again be more fairly represented. When preaching is a bit arrogant, pushy, assertive, incomprehensible, then our medium will more appropriately fit with the message, and the gospel will be more fairly proclaimed.

I recall a passage in Richard Baxter's *The Reformed Pastor*:

It is most desirable that the minister should be of parts above the people so far as to be able to teach them, and awe them. See that you preach to such auditors as these some higher points that stall their understandings, and feed them not with all milk but sometimes with stronger meat; for it exceedingly puffs them up with pride when they hear nothing from ministers but that they know already or can say themselves. . . . Not that I would have you neglect the great fundamental verities, or wrong the weak and ignorant people while you are dealing with such as these; but only when the main part of your sermons is as plain as you can speak, let some one small part be such as shall puzzle these self-conceited men; or else have one sermon in four or five on purpose for them . . . and let them see that it is not your obscure manner of handling but the matter itself that is too hard for them, and so may see that they are yet but children that have need of milk, and that you would be more upon such higher points if it were not that their incapacity doth take you off.[18]

Walter Brueggemann says, "The preacher must have a larger vision of what a sermon intends to do, so that there is a long-term strategy about the 'human predicament' and the 'evangelical possibility' that are juxtaposed in the sermon."[19]

Preachers must keep before themselves a larger vision; otherwise sermons will, over time, degenerate into the conventional and the expected. Various symptoms of the crisis among us catch our attention. Ecological destruction, domestic violence, poverty. It is not the preacher's task first to argue that one symptom is worse than another, like competing caucuses at General Conference. The preacher's first task is to help us to articulate our symptoms theologically, through baptismal speech, speech that might sometimes, in Baxter's words, "stall the understanding."

18. In Thomas Wood, ed., *Five Pastorals* (London: SPCK, 1961), p. 233.
19. Brueggemann, p. 25.

We were being pounded by the storm so violently that on the next day they began to throw the cargo overboard, and on the third day with their own hands they threw the ship's tackle overboard. When neither sun nor stars appeared for many days, and no small tempest raged, all hope of our being saved was at last abandoned. . . . Just before daybreak, Paul urged all of them to take some food, saying, "Today is the fourteenth day that you have been in suspense and remaining without food, having eaten nothing. Therefore I urge you to take some food, for it will help you survive." . . . After he had said this, he took bread; and giving thanks to God in the presence of all, he broke it and began to eat. Then all of them were encouraged and took food for themselves." (Acts 27:18-20; 33-36, NRSV)

John the Baptist invited us to come, be washed, sign on with the kingdom. Jesus' invitation was even more radical. Come, wade into the sea, die, be drowned and re-created, be those who break bread in the middle of the storm. So Dorothy Day, whose life embodied such radical turning, spoke of the love of God as "a harsh and dreadful love."

I had given a talk on baptism. She said, "I was a Southern Baptist. We baptized people, and that church was where I encountered racism and sexism. Your claims for baptism are a bit too simplistic for me."

True. The baptizers have not always been faithful to their own claims for the baptized. However, one of our claims is that baptism is also about repentance — daily, painful turning from sin and toward God. Baptism is a one-time event that takes our whole life to finish.

"And would that you did reign. . . . For I think that God has exhibited us apostles as last of all, like people sentenced to death" (1 Corinthians 4:8-9).

"Divine Divestment"

Twenty-first Sunday after Pentecost
Mark 10:17-27

T HE Danish philosopher, Søren Kierkegaard, came home
after church one Sunday and wrote of his disgust at what
happened there:

> In the magnificent cathedral the Honourable and Right
> Reverend Geheime-General Ober-Hof Pradikant, the elect
> favourite of the fashionable world, appears before an elect
> company and preaches with emotion upon the text he
> himself elected: "God hath elected the base things of the
> world, and the things that are despised" *and nobody laughs.*
> (*Attack Upon Christendom, 1944*)

Today I am to preach on Mark 10:17-27. The story of Jesus
and the Rich Man. Rick Lischer, Professor of Preaching at the
Divinity School, was supposed to preach on this text. I
thought that I asked him to preach on this text on this day.
Two weeks ago Rick told me that he had not heard about
it, had never received a letter from me, and was planning to
be at his fortieth high school reunion. That is no excuse. He
was supposed to preach on this text. Now *I* have to preach
on this text. I had to leave my beach house yesterday, get

in my $15,000 car, and drive to my $150,000 home, in order to preach to you on this text. I wonder if, when I am done, any of you will laugh.

Let us put this episode in context. Jesus has just blessed children (10:13-16). Jesus was lecturing away one day, everybody trying to pay attention, everybody taking notes on his theology lecture. But his disciples said, "Master, send these children away."

They were being distracted by the children. Somebody had pulled somebody else's hair. Somebody was rolling around in the dirt, wrestling with somebody else. "Master, send these children away."

Do you remember what Jesus did on that occasion? Mark says that he took a child and placed the child in the midst of them. In other words, this helpless, small, ignorant, vulnerable, and dependent little child, the one whom we in our society place at the margins of our society, Jesus put in the midst of them. We put children out on the fringes of our society. After all, they are unproductive, dependent, and vulnerable. We have progressed to the point where our society treats its very young and its very old the same way: namely, we institutionalize them. We put them away in institutions and pay people to look after them. After all, both the very young and the very old make no contribution to society: they are unproductive, dependent, *small*.

The curious thing is that Jesus took those whom we put at the fringe of society and put them right in the middle of the disciples. Those whom we regard as distraction from the really important things, Jesus put in the middle of us in a last ditch effort to help us pay attention.

It is as if Jesus wanted to say, "You want to get into my kingdom? The only way to get into my kingdom is to be very small, very little, very needy. There will be no adults in my kingdom, no self-sufficient, liberated, autonomous, inde-

68

pendent adults. There will only be children. Here is a kingdom that has a very small door."

At any rate, Jesus has just shocked the disciples by pulling
a child out of the crowd and putting the child in the midst
of them.

As fate would have it, this episode is followed by another
in which anything but a little, weak, needy, dependent, and
small child comes forth to Jesus. Mark says that the person
who came to Jesus was "a rich man." Matthew, when he tells
the story, says that he was "young." Luke says that he was
a "ruler." But all three Gospels agree that, whether he is
young, a ruler, or what, *he is rich.*

This rich man comes to Jesus saying that he wants some
of this "Eternal Life" Jesus has to offer. Evidently, despite the
fact that he is rich, despite his having many things, he doesn't
have "Eternal Life." So he asked Jesus, "What must *I do* to
have eternal life?"

What must I do (evidently, he has been very successful at
his doing) to get eternal life. "Eternal Life" is just another way
of saying "kingdom of God" in Mark's Gospel. "How can I get
into your kingdom," asked the young man who has been very
successful at getting to the top of this world's kingdom.

Jesus responds, "You want to get into this kingdom?
Simple. All you have to do to get in God's kingdom is to
obey all of the commandments. Don't worship anything but
God, don't commit adultery, don't steal, don't lie, don't kill,
don't be envious of anything anybody else has, keep the
Sabbath, stuff like that."

Robert Capon says that in invoking the anything-but-
simple-to-follow Ten Commandments, Jesus expected this
high achiever to recoil and say something like, "Gosh, Jesus,
when you put it like that, why in the world should I be
going out looking for something else to do, when I have
done such a lousy job of doing the things that I have already
been commanded to do?"

But this young man was a hard-core success. So he replied, "Gosh, Jesus, I have done all that since I was a kid in Sunday School." Evidently, this young man is a bigger success than even Jesus thought. He has not only been successful at getting material things but he has been a spiritual success as well.

In the context of that day, the young man's success at keeping the Ten Commandments would not be that surprising. After all, because he is rich, he has plenty of free time on his hands, plenty of time to study the Bible and to do what the Bible commands. If he needs to take all weekend off to study the Bible, go to church, and do good things, he can afford it. It was believed that rich people had been blessed by God. One way they had been blessed is with enough free time to be a success at religion.

I very well remember the woman who told me, when I urged her to come to my church, that she found it difficult to come to church on Sunday morning. When I asked her why, she rather embarrassingly explained, "Look, I am a waitress. I work ten hours a day, six days a week as a waitress. On Sunday morning, when I wake up, I can hardly get out of bed. Worse, my feet are so swollen, I cannot get on my Sunday shoes. That's why I don't come to church."

Because they thought that the rich were blessed with enough free time to read and obey the Bible, hire expensive psychotherapists, go to affluent universities, and ponder the mysteries of life, you can imagine their shock when Jesus turns to this materially and spiritually rich young man and says, "So you have succeeded in obeying the Ten Commandments? Then let me ask you to do just one teeny weeny little thing for me. Go, sell all you have, and give it to the poor, and come follow me and you will have treasure in heaven."

To everybody's amazement, Jesus considered the young man's wealth, not as a sign of divine favor, but as a big problem.

"Strip down, raffle your Porsche, liquidate your portfolio,

break free and give it all to the poor." In other words, strip down, throw away your crutches, become weak, little, small, poor, and vulnerable. You can't get in here, unless you come as a little child. Didn't I say this kingdom has a very small door?

With that, Mark says, the young man slumped down, got real depressed, got into his Porsche, and drove away.

You see, this is a *call story*. It is very similar to other call stories in the Gospel of Mark (1:16-20; 2:14; 10:46-52). Someone is being invited to join up with Jesus and become a disciple. Interestingly enough, in those stories of Jesus' call and invitation, people come forth and follow. In this story, the man walks away. He walks away because he is rich.

As he is walking away, Jesus turns to his disciples (10:23-27), to us, to the church, and says out loud, "Man, it is really hard to get one of these rich ones into my kingdom."

One of the disciples says, "How hard is it, Jesus?"

Jesus says, "It's hard. In fact, I would say it is about as hard for one of these rich people to get into my kingdom as to shove a camel through the eye of a needle."

That hard!

Can you see why I wanted Rick Lischer to preach on this text and not me? Let's face it, by the standards of that day, by the standards of this day, we know where we would find our place in this story. *We* are the rich young man. He is us all over.

Anuradhi Vittachi (*Earth Conference One*, 1989) asks us to imagine the world as a village with one hundred families:

If this metaphorical village consists of one hundred families . . . sixty-five cannot read. Some eighty families have no members who have flown on airplanes, and seventy have no drinking water at home. About sixty families occupy ten percent of the village, while just seven own sixty percent of the land. . . . Only one family has a university education.

71

The rich young man is us all over.

And I really wish I could help you out of this "easier for a camel to get through the eye of a needle than for a rich person to enter the kingdom" text. Creative homiletical attempts to change one Greek letter so that the word will not be "camel" but rather "rope" will not work. Jesus said camel, not rope. (Besides, it would be no easy thing to get a rope through the eye of a needle anyway!) Around the ninth century, some creative preacher claimed that there was a gate in Jerusalem named "The Needle's Eye" so that Jesus was talking about how difficult it was to get a fully loaded camel through this relatively narrow gate. No, that is an invention of a preacher like me who, back in the ninth century, probably had to preach this text to a congregation like us.

The disciples spoke for us all, "God! Who can be saved?"

And Jesus replies, "It's hard. It's hard. Impossible, for rich people to enter the kingdom. In fact, it is impossible for *anybody* to enter this kingdom. But with God, all things are possible, even this."

Just in case you watched the previous episode with Jesus receiving and blessing the little child (10:13-16) and thought that it was a sweet, nice, easy thing to come to Jesus, Mark records this. We can only come to Jesus as a small, needy, little child. But there is nothing sweet or nice about it. It's hard.

As a preacher, I must not make this sound easy. It's hard. In fact, it is impossible. Then Jesus says, *"With God, even this is possible."* It is even possible for someone who is rich to divest and get into the kingdom. And I don't know whether that is good news or bad. Jesus has clearly taught that you can only come into this kingdom as a child, as someone who is needy, small, and poor. How can we come into this kingdom when we are all big, grown up, self-sufficient, well-to-do, and scored high on the SAT? Jesus says, "With

God it is possible." That is, with God, it is possible that, given enough time, *we* will get stripped down, made small, impoverished, divested.

With God, that is possible? This world's kingdoms belong to those who sing "I Am Just a Material Girl," and "It's Money That Matters." You can't imagine the possibility of our being able to let go, strip down, and divest of those things to which we so ruthlessly cling in this life. But with God, Jesus promises, it may just be possible. *And I don't know whether that is a promise or a threat.*

As we go through life, getting our advanced degrees, earning our salaries, driving our cars, paying our mortgages, we had better look over our shoulder. When we get all secure, set-up, insured, and well-fixed, there may be that old Pursuer behind us, just waiting to jump us in order to divest us. With God, it's possible. Lamar Williamson says, "If this message does not take our breath away, if we are not shocked, grieved, or amazed, we have either not yet heard it or heard it so often that we do not really hear it anymore."

After we spiritualize it, explain it away, this text sits there, grinning at us. It looks around at us all. We exclaim, "It's hard! Who then can be saved?" With God it may be possible.

She went to Honduras with the Duke Chapel Mission team on her spring break. Went to help the poor in Honduras, spent her spring break living with a poor family in the mountains of Honduras, sleeping on a dirt floor, living without electricity or running water.

In the evenings she sat with the family in the twilight, singing, listening to stories around the fire. In that family, the elders were cherished, the children were adored.

"That family," she said later, "made me think of my family. Compared with that family in Honduras, my family is dysfunctional. Why is it that we have so much, yet have so little of what matters?"

She went to Honduras to help the poor and surprise! she

73

got helped. She went there rich; she returned poor. Which is good news because Jesus says, nobody who's rich and big can get into his kingdom. But then this good news: With God even the impossible is possible. Or is this bad news? You make the call.

As Athol Gill sums it up in *Life on the Road:*

This is the only time in the gospels that we are specifically told of a person declining the call of Jesus — and, let the Western church mark and understand, he does so because of his material possessions! Yet Mark records the fact simply and unemotionally. The young man who had such great potential disappears from the stage and we hear nothing more about him. Even his name has been forgotten.

C. S. Lewis once noted, "Now all things are possible. All things are possible. It is even possible to get a large camel through the small eye of a needle. That's possible. *But it will be extremely hard on the camel."*

3

Preaching to Pagans

WHEN John the Baptist appeared preaching, he came preaching good news (*evangelion*). No doubt, for many who heard The Baptist, John's news did not sound so good. After all, it was good news about repentance. John's preaching was directed at the children of Abraham, Israel. He spoke within the narrative framework of a people who expected God to intervene, to make their history God's own, a God who saves. Our description of preaching as speech among and to the baptized thus fits the depiction of John the Baptist's preaching at the beginning of the Gospels and Jesus' preaching in Nazareth in Luke 4. We preach, like John or Jesus, among the family, bringing to speech that which has happened in our baptism.

Yet this depiction sketches the church-world distinction in too neat a dichotomy. The baptized who gather on Sunday are also creatures of the world. We speak (in my congregation) English. We are formed not only by baptism but by a host of other masters. Is not our talk about the distinctiveness of baptismal discourse called into question by the presence of so much of "the world" in the church on Sunday? Biblical illiteracy, cultural pluralism, all of the linguistic and theological compromises we have made in our church's interface with the world suggest to some that the best hope for Christian preachers is to find some sort of religious *Esperanto,* a culturally approved common mode of discourse, a meta-language that frees us from the linguistic bind imposed upon us by having to work with pre–second-century Hebrew and Greek texts.

For most sermons I hear, and too many that I preach, this is exactly what we have done. Biblical apocalyptic is existentialized, biblical prophecy is moralized, biblical narrative is psychologized, all in the interest of enabling our worldly hearers to take us seriously. We hope, we preachers, that there may be some place for us to stand that is not linguistically qualified by baptism, some way for our sermons to make sense apart from a church that makes them make sense.

Baptism makes our claims sound so parochial (literally, tied to the parish), so arrogant in the face of the fact of worldwide religious pluralism. In a dangerously divided world, wouldn't our time as preachers be better spent in the search for some common universal, linguistic denominator rather than in renewed cultivation of the distinctiveness of Christian discourse? Doesn't it seem a bit odd that Christians should persist in defending the superiority of our truth claims in the face of a culture in which there are now more Moslems than Episcopalians? (A particularly devastating observation in a denomination like mine [United Methodist] in which truth appears to be determined by majority vote.) Should we not at least try to make statements like, "Jesus Christ is Lord," with a bit more humility, acknowledging that all truth is relative? And isn't there some way to translate these tough texts so they don't require our having to submit to conversion? Even to ask the question is to show that we have aleady been converted to a world that is not Christian.

On Refusing to Take the World as It Is

Behind all these universalizing proposals is the assumption that the "world" is more wide and more public than the church. Church talk is "in house" speech, whereas worldly talk is "public." Our task as preachers, if we want to be heard by those in the world, is to adjust our parochial, "in house" ecclesial speech to the talk of the "wider world."

Two Christian ethicists recently argued for a revival of "public theology" by first saying that "All politics and all economics must be conducted under the context-transcending principles of truth, justice, and love." Then they urge Christians to "reach beyond confessional particularities, exclusive histories and privileged realms of discourse" or Christians will merely "preach to their choirs." "This agenda for Christian thought requires a 'public theology,' a way of speaking about the reality of God and God's will for the world that is intellectually valid in the marketplace of ideas and morally effective in the marketplace of goods and services."[1] It is rather amazing that someone still thinks words like "truth, justice, and love" are "context-transcending principles." Try talking with a Marxist, a Buddhist, or a Jew about "justice" and you will see what I mean. There is no privileged domain of "public" discourse that will save us from having to define our terms. When we do define them, we will discover that there are no terms that are not context (i.e., story) dependent. Of course I doubt that these two ethicists really want to talk to Buddhists or to Jews. Their audience, the "public" they long for theology to address in an "intellectually valid" way, is secular, technological, national economics. They want Christians, Jews, and Buddhists to lay aside our "confessional particularities" and "exclusive histories" in order to be culturally significant in the

1. Max L. Stackhouse and Dennis P. McCann, "Public Theology after the Collapse of Socialism," *The Christian Century*, Jan. 16, 1991, p. 45.

only valid culture, namely, the secular, nationally determined ones. They name their world as a "marketplace of ideas." Forgive Christians for wanting to name the world as something other than K-Mart.

The greatest arrogance of contemporary liberal democracy is its arrogant presumption that its values and its language are unconditioned by stories, contexts, and cultures while everyone else's language is parochial and contextualized. Reference to "truth, justice, and love" are, far from being a way to transcend our nasty particularities of being Christian, Jew, Moslem, or atheist, merely demands that we all submit to conversion into secular, godless, Western liberals before we are allowed to speak.

This theology has not gone public, it has merely capitulated and been converted by another "theology." No wonder that when this sort of "public theology" speaks to the "wider world" it is generally ignored. It has gone public in a desperate attempt to speak to a world that can hear what this "public theology" has to say from any number of other sources without having to bother itself with the baggage of residual Christianity. The "public" it addresses is confined to the liberal democracies of the industrialized West.

George Orwell, examining the political power of language, noted that many silly things are uttered in the speech of modern Western intellectuals. Silly things are uttered, to be sure, largely because we have foolish thoughts — "But the slovenliness of our language makes it easier for us to have foolish thoughts." Orwell complained that "as soon as certain topics are raised [like religion, economics, or politics?], the concrete melts into the abstract and no one seems able to think. . . ."[2] Most good preachers know the stifling smog

---

2. George Orwell, "Politics and the English Language," in *Shooting an Elephant and Other Essays* (New York: Harcourt, Brace, Jovanovich, 1945), pp. 28, 29.

that hovers over a congregation when abstractions like "truth, justice, and love" flow from the pulpit.

So Stackhouse and McCann urge us to "rediscover these resources" within "Protestant and Catholic communities of faith" or else be relegated to "irrelevance" (p. 47). I daresay that the gospel demands to be considerably more than a mere "resource" to keep Western culture afloat. Besides, if we Christians really do have something to offer for the good of the culture, why then must the culture silence us *as Christians?* Why cannot the gospel and its claims be every bit as "intellectually valid" as capitalism?

By speaking in terms of "public theology" and the "wider world," we have set up the problem in such a way as to suggest that Christian communicators have two options: (1) content ourselves with "in house" speech among the baptized *cognoscenti* ("preaching to the choir"); or (2) find some new language that will enable us to be understood in the "marketplace of ideas" by the "wider" world. Yet the wider world, as John Yoder reminds us in *The Priestly Kingdom,* is still a small place which speaks only one language at a time.[3] All language is "in house" speech. That which we privilege with the name "wider society" is not the universe. No language transcends its communal particularity, even though its particular community enables it to use words like "universal," "humanity," "justice," and so on. When a preacher disposes of baptismal speech in favor of psychological speech (Robert Schuller's "Be Happy Attitudes" or "Self-Esteem"), or secular politicized speech (mainline Protestantism's "Peace with Justice"), the preacher has not thereby transcended the community-bound nature of language. The preacher has merely moved, in speech, from one community to another.

So back to our initial homiletical concern. How can the

3. John Howard Yoder, *The Priestly Kingdom* (Notre Dame, Ind.: University of Notre Dame Press, 1984), chap. 2.

particular, narratively and ecclesially conditioned truths of the baptismal community be proclaimed in a public world that does not share those truths?

Fortunately, the question is an old one, at least as old as the New Testament. The church came into being as a message that had to be carried from one community to another. Born in tiny Aramaic communities, in less than two centuries after its birth in Judaea, the church's peculiar brand of messianism was flourishing in Rome. Moving rapidly from the insular, persecuted, occupied culture of Judaea, the good news had caused enough havoc in pluralistic Rome to merit official persecution. Christians were persecuted by the otherwise tolerant and pluralistic Romans because Rome had the good sense to recognize in this new Judaean splinter group a threat to the religious status quo of the Empire. If these Christians could have been linguistically assimilated, then they would not have needed to be murdered.

Christian communicators readily used the Greek language that was available to them. Yet they did not accept the cosmology, the world which Greek language conventionally described. The language was seized and used for a very different message in order to construe for the hearers a very different world. I have no way of substantiating that claim other than through a story:

> While Paul was waiting for them in Athens, he was deeply distressed to see that the city was full of idols. So he argued in the synagogue with the Jews and the devout persons, and also in the marketplace every day with those who happened to be there. Also some Epicurean and Stoic philosophers debated with him. Some said, "What does this babbler want to say?" Others said, "He seems to be a proclaimer of foreign divinities." (This was because he was telling the good news about Jesus and the resurrection.) So they took him and brought him to the Areopagus and

asked him, "May we know what this new teaching is that you are presenting? It sounds rather strange to us, so we would like to know what it means." Now all the Athenians and the foreigners living there would spend their time in nothing but telling or hearing something new.

Then Paul stood in front of the Areopagus and said, "Athenians, I see how extremely religious you are in every way. For as I went through the city and looked carefully at the objects of your worship, I found among them an altar with the inscription, 'To an unknown god.' What therefore you worship as unknown, this I proclaim to you. The God who made the world and everything in it, he who is Lord of heaven and earth, does not live in shrines made by human hands, nor is he served by human hands, as though he needed anything, since he himself gives to all mortals life and breath and all things. From one ancestor he made all nations to inhabit the whole earth, and he allotted the times of their existence and the boundaries of the places where they would live, so that they would search for God and perhaps grope for him and find him — though indeed he is not far from each one of us. For 'In him we live and move and have our being'; as even some of your own poets have said,

'For we too are his offspring.'

Since we are God's offspring, we ought not to think that the deity is like gold, or silver, or stone, an image formed by the art and imagination of mortals. While God has overlooked the times of human ignorance, now he commands all people everywhere to repent, because he has fixed a day on which he will have the world judged in righteousness by a man whom he has appointed, and of this he has given assurance to all by raising him from the dead.

81

When they heard of the resurrection of the dead, some scoffed; but others said, "We will hear you again about this." At that point Paul left them. But some of them joined him and became believers, including Dionysius the Areopagite and a woman named Damaris and others with them. (Acts 17:16-34)

The paradigmatic instance of Christian speaking in public is Luke's story of Paul on the Areopagus in Acts 17:16-34. By this point in Luke's Acts of the Apostles, we have seen the power of the gospel to reach rich and poor, Jew and Gentile, slave and free, male and female. But can the gospel hold its own in the sophisticated intellectual environment of a university town? Luke takes Paul to Athens, to the heart of the very best of pagan culture, the town of Pericles and Plato.[4]

Frankly, Paul is unimpressed. The sculptures of Phidias move him not. Good Jew that he is, Paul sees Athens as little more than a wasteland "full of idols" (17:16). He argues with Jews, Epicureans, and Stoics, even those who look down their academic noses at this "babbler" (verse 18). Here is obviously a very public communicator, this Paul, a preacher who is quite eager to argue with anyone in whatever world he finds himself. Others, after much research and careful investigation, come to the stunning discovery that "he seems to be a preacher of foreign divinities" (verse 18), perhaps thinking to absorb whatever new gods Paul brings into their polytheistic pantheon of exotic gods (crypto-pluralism!). After all, they are not closed minded. Paul pursues their legendary Athenian curiosity into the Areopagus where the Athenians spent their days doing what intellectuals enjoy — relieving their boredom by searching for new ideas. Despite the fact that Luke spends much of his time in Luke/Acts demonstrat-

4. See my *Acts* in the series Interpretation: A Bible Commentary for Teaching and Preaching (Atlanta: John Knox, 1988), pp. 142-44.

ing that Jesus, as the fulfillment of the promises made to
Israel, is anything but new, for the Athenians Jesus' novelty
attracts their attention more quickly than truth. The pluralism
inherent in paganism appears to have a virtually limitless
ability to absorb all ideas and conflicting belief systems into
itself, baptizing all truth claims on the basis that all truth is
new, relative, and therefore to be tolerated as personal
opinion rather than fact.

The Athenian setting gives Luke an opportunity for a
demonstration of the possibilities and pitfalls of an evangelistic appeal to Christianity's cultured despisers, the alleged "wider world." Here is the only speech in the book
of Acts made to Gentiles by the missionary to the Gentiles
(who seems otherwise to prefer debating texts with Jews).
In a well-constructed piece of classical rhetoric, Paul, por-
trayed here by Luke as a virtual Christian Socrates, first
flatters his audience (verses 22-23). Idolaters they may be,
but at least they are searching, at least their impulse to
worship is right even if the objects of their worship are
wrong. He has seen their altar to "an unknown god" (verse
23). Their religious yearning, even though a bit of a scandal
to a monotheistic Jew, is the inarticulate and uninformed
yearning of the pagan for the God that only the Scriptures
can disclose.

Or is Paul mocking the Athenians here? When Paul tells
them that he perceives that they are "extremely religious,"
does he mean this as compliment or as criticism? Throughout
Acts, Gentiles are shown to be incurably religious. That is,
a Gentile will worship anything — gold, silver, sex, wood,
the military, money — if given half a chance to worship
something. (When Cornelius meets Peter in Acts 10:25, he
tries to worship Peter. When Paul and Barnabas heal a man
at Lystra, the whole town names them as gods and tries to
worship them [Acts 14:8-20]. Gentiles are very religious.)
Good Jew that he is, Paul knows that our chief human

problem is not atheism but idolatry. We are all "extremely religious." Idolatry comes to us quite naturally.

We hear echoes at this point of Paul's reflection upon the pilgrimage of pagans to the Christ that he records in 1 Thessalonians 1:9-10. Appealing to the Athenians' knowledge of creation (for he could not simply recite Scripture to pagans who were ignorant of Scripture) and to our common humanity, Paul asserts that his great God "made the world and everything in it" (verse 24). This great God cannot be captured in "shrines made by human hands" (verse 24) but exists over the face of the whole earth that we all might find our true purpose in his service alone (verses 28-29). Until now, pagan ignorance was overlooked, but now is the time to turn toward the one true God who has not only created the inhabitants of the world but also shall judge them (verse 31). In this reasoning from the natural world toward faith in God, Luke's Paul borders upon a "natural theology" — our observation of the natural world and its wonders is a forerunner of faith.

How can people look up at the stars, or ponder the mysteries of life in the world without imagining a real, though still unknown divine force behind it all? In citing the verses of a pagan poet (verse 28), in drawing upon the pagan's experience of the world, Paul hopes to move them toward faith by way of the natural world. (Although elsewhere Paul used natural theology not to appeal to pagans, but to condemn pagan sinfulness — Romans 1:18.)

Yet Paul cannot convert his audience through an appeal to their observation of the world. Paul's claims are more confrontal and subversive than they first appear. Little in classical paganism (other than late Roman cynicism) justifies an assault upon the gods. Revelation takes us where observation alone cannot go. Too many people look at growing grass and see only cells dividing, or into the sky and see bits of matter and swirling balls of gas. Natural theology is no more than preliminary instruction. Something else is needed. Paul asserts the resurrection — a fact completely contrary to our observation of the way the world works. In nature, things die, decay, decline. Death is death. What is done is done, over and finished, ended. Yet Paul concludes his speech with the assertion that, for Christians, the resurrection of Jesus is our "assurance." Not grass growing in spring, the return of the robin, the opening of the cocoon, or any other naturalistic drivel; the resurrection, something beyond the natural, is the final assurance that this one is "Lord of heaven and earth" (17:24).

In mentioning the judgment and the resurrection, Paul risks rejection by his audience. They may agree to a created world and to our common humanity, but there is no possible "natural theology" evidence for an assertion of the resurrection. There is no evidence that our actions shall be judged by an authority higher than our own opinions. His assertion of judgment may even be a more radical claim than his assertion of the resurrection. Appeals to reason and to observation of the natural world are risky in the proclamation of the gospel. Eventually revelation must be invoked and the scandal of faith both to pagan reason and pagan experience must be made plain. Of course, it is not that Paul denies the value of both "reason" and "experience." It is rather that Paul asserts some very un-pagan definitions of reason and experience.

The response to Paul's address is much the same as he encountered elsewhere: some mocked (verse 32), others believed (verse 34), including two Athenian nobles and a woman (what kind of community is this that remembers a woman's name?).

Christian proclamation is not to be judged merely by its success in winning an approving response. Where the Word is faithfully preached, some believe, some mock. Even Paul's oratorical skill cannot remove the offense of the gospel — in fact, it accentuates it.

85

Calvin charged that "the human mind is a perpetual factory for idols." Idolatry is not necessarily the pastime of the ignorant and the simple. Intellectuals play quite well at this game. Natural inquisitiveness and delight in the novel and the strange, so prevalent in the academy, can be little more than the itch for some new graven image. The God whom Paul proclaims is not just another option for human devotion, not a pluralistic God content to be one among many. The God who sent the Christ is still the Holy One of Israel, a jealous deity without rivals, an exclusive lover who tolerates no competition — money, sex, philosophical ideals, institutions — who fiercely judges all idols made by human hands or minds. Christian speakers do not just massage the world as we find it. We create a new world.

On Taking the World Seriously

In Acts 17:16-34, Luke has become fully at home within the linguistic world of paganism, facing its questions and using its speech. Luke refuses, however, to fit the good news of Jesus into paganism's preconceived categories. Jesus Christ is Lord. This means that Jesus does not simply fit into the already available world; he is both above the cosmos and in charge of it. Pagans, no less than Christians, sought some key to the cosmos, some means — cultic, philosophical, or otherwise — of fitting into the powers that be. If we cannot control the stars, we can at least understand the stars whose movements control us. Even though Nancy Reagan's astrological yearning is the beginning of this exercise in public communication, it cannot be the end, because the Christian good news has some very definite and very countercultural things to say about the "powers that be" that judge and reform our desire to know and to control those powers.

It is also important to note that, while this Christian encounter with paganism attempts to speak to pagans, it in no way leaves Judaism behind. What is proclaimed here, even though there are real difficulties in enabling pagans to understand it, is within the scope of messianic Judaism. Not being content to be relegated to the position of just one more truth option within classical pagan pluralism, the church now claimed that the ancient Hebrew story had, through an amazing act of God in Christ, widened to include everyone. Whereas the Baptist proclaimed a God who called Israel down to the Jordan to repent and be washed, Paul at Athens proclaims the good news that God now "commands all people everywhere to repent" (Acts 17:30). The story that had begun by asserting God's graciousness in forming a new people, Israel, had continued to embrace all peoples, or so Paul claimed.

What we are witnessing here is a group of Jews who have received a message that compels them to move out beyond the confines of their somewhat defensive society to assault the intellectual bastions of the majority pagan culture. They, like Paul on the Areopagus, refused to contextualize their good news by clothing it within the philosophical categories already available to them. Their good news was more than an embellishment, a corrective, or a complement to what well-educated pagans in Athens already knew. The judgment of God upon humanity, the resurrection of Jesus from the dead, signified an assault upon conventional cosmology. That assault, and its embrace of the whole world, was rooted in and understandable from the context of God's dealings with Israel. To speak to these Gentiles did not mean abandoning the story of God and Israel. That story was the basis for the conversation.

Lesslie Newbigin presents a three-part missionary pattern for witnessing to any culture with the gospel. First, Newbigin says that missionary speaking must occur in the language of the receptor culture, accepting at least in a provisional way

87

the way of understanding the world that is embodied in that language. Second, missionary communication will call radically into question that culture's understanding of reality, which is both expressed and formed by its language, with an unashamed call for repentance, a call to, in Newbigin's words, make "a U-turn of the mind." And third, if the receptors do experience faith, repentance, and conversion, it is nothing less than a miracle, a work of God, not the result of the communicator's competency.[5] In speaking of Christ within any culture, Newbigin says that a Christian evangelist must find a way between two dangers:

> On the one hand, he may simply fail to communicate: he uses the words of the language, but in such a way that he sounds like a foreigner; his message is heard as the babblings of a man who really has nothing to say. Or, on the other hand, he may so far succeed in talking the language of his hearers that he is accepted all too easily as a familiar character — a moralist calling for greater purity of conduct or a guru offering a path to the salvation that all human beings want. His message is simply absorbed into the existing world-view and heard as a call to be more pious or better behaved. In the attempt to be "relevant" one may fall into syncretism, and in the effort to avoid syncretism one may become irrelevant. (p. 7)

I have been grateful for the way in which Newbigin has recovered the notion of Christian communication as a clash of cultures. I wish that, in his books on missionary proclamation of the gospel, Newbigin had given greater stress to the role of the community, the church, as source and destination of that proclamation; nevertheless, Newbigin's insights

---

5. Lesslie Newbigin, *Foolishness to the Greeks: The Gospel and Western Culture*, (Grand Rapids: Eerdmans, 1986), pp. 1-11.

are rich for us preachers. Having learned to communicate the gospel in the mission setting, Newbigin was among the first to help us name contemporary North America as the newest of the church's mission fields.

Evangelical preaching occurs whenever a Christian communicator confesses the invasion of God into our history, the assault of God upon our cosmologies begun in Israel, now graciously continued in the church. This good news is news because others cannot know it unless someone tells them. This good news is good because hearing it brings about true freedom. It cannot be communicated coercively, for it must be received as good news rather than as compulsion. Its reception cannot be guaranteed because good news does not come naturally to us. It is a gift, grace.

When we speak of the problem of communicating the good news to the world, we must do so within this evangelical context. When we speak about what has happened in Christ, we do so as messengers of good news. "What therefore you worship as unknown, this I proclaim to you" (Acts 17:23).

When we proclaim the good news to the world, we do not claim that people who have not heard this news are bad people. They simply are those who have not heard this news. This is their news because the good news is news about the whole world. It is news that the world is much more interesting than the pagan world of cause-effect, nature cycles, and a squabbling host of deities. What Paul proclaimed in Athens is the news that the world is the meaningful product of a purposeful Creator who loves to talk and who is determined to include all in the conversation.

The homiletical, evangelical question for early Christian communicators was not, Should we use Greek? or Should we utilize Hellenistic concepts and to what degree? The question was, *How shall we be a sign, signal, and witness to the world that Jesus Christ is Lord?*

89

The world does not naturally affirm the sovereignty of Christ. Monotheism does not come naturally. Sovereignty must be announced, enacted by the presence of a counter-cultural community that is itself evidence for such sovereignty. Paul had to communicate Christ's sovereignty within a pagan, Greek-speaking world. We must communicate with a pagan world of pluralism and relativism. We need not copy Paul's manner of speaking, but we ought to emulate Paul's pushy assertion of the shape of the world. We cannot concede the adequacy of the ideas currently dominating the discussion of the allegedly "wider world," and we refuse to concede that we are not every bit as "public" in our speaking as nationalistic liberals.

I remember the friend of mine who returned from a visit to the Soviet Union in the 1970s (on a trip sponsored by the National Council of Churches) announcing to us that the church was mostly "irrelevant because the only people there are little old ladies." Looking back now at the collapse of communism, the embarrassment of those seminary professors who advocated this god as the savior for Latin America, the difficulties of rebuilding the Soviet Union after a long period of spiritual bankruptcy, I hope my friend would now say "thank God for the little old ladies." They bet on the stronger of two gods and won. Their existence provided a continuing, visible, political rebuke to the Soviets. (In 1990, a group representing the United Methodist Church gave Mr. Gorbachev the United Methodist "Peacemaker of the Year Award." Four months later, Mr. Gorbachev sent tanks to crush the Baltic Republics. I hope that we will ask him to return the award. It rightfully belongs to those "little old ladies.") The church subverts the given world order by forming a new one, and those "little old ladies" are our chief means of subversion.

By its own rules of grammar, modern relativism will not enable us to say "Jesus Christ is Lord." It does not know how

90

to handle such assertion. However, we Christians are not frightened by the modern recognition of the relativity of truth. Relativity might be another way of saying that all truth is historically, communally, narratively conditioned, a claim that Christianity exemplified long before modern philosophers thought of it. To believe otherwise is to believe an assertion of Greek philosophy (the universality of ideas) that has been decisively defeated in our own age. When Paul claimed that the world and all that was in it was the creation of the God of Israel, he did not do so on any universal, allegedly nonrelativized basis. He did so on the basis of the faith revealed to Israel. From out of the words and experiences of this particular ragtag band of nomads called Israel were God's purposes for the whole cosmos revealed, which is about as relativistic an origin for cosmic claims as one can imagine. It is also about as universal a claim as could be imagined, for it announces that what God did in Jesus of Nazareth, God has done for the whole world.

Whatever we say, it must take the form of witness, of proclamation. We can only testify to what we have seen and heard. We can signify the good news in the water and the word of baptism. We can, in our congregational life together, witness that God really has formed a new people. We cannot coerce the hearer with arguments. Paul's experience in Athens warns us to expect rejection, possibly meager results.

Yet the good news in our struggles to proclaim the good news is that, whenever we stand up to proclaim, in Athens, Greece, or Athens, Georgia, we are standing on our own ground. This world is not the wider world in distinction from the more narrow world of the church. This world is Christ's. "The kingdom of the world has become the kingdom of our Lord and of his Christ, and he shall reign for ever and ever" (Revelation 11:15).

When Paul spoke Greek on the Areopagus, he was laying claim to another corner of enemy territory for its true Lord.

He was participating in the mopping up action after the decisive victory of Easter. When we modern Christians embrace relativism and openly admit that our truth claims are relative to the existence and witness of Israel, we are merely embracing a philosophical spin-off of the early claim that Jesus Christ is Lord. His Lordship has relativized all principalities and powers and put them under his feet.

Relativism is a threat, and a big threat to the impulse that raised the questions at the beginning of this discussion on preaching to pagans. To repeat: is our best option, as contemporary communicators of the gospel, to "find some new language that will enable us to be understood by the wider world"?

The question itself is a result of our relinquishing political and social authority to a particular system of belief that is most helpful to the establishment's maintenance of the status quo. The established order has a stake in fostering a dream of monocultural unity (a "new world order") that removes all subjective choice and the particularities of history. The Empire needs to convince all ethnic groups, all religious enclaves, that they exist apart from something the establishment calls "the wider world." The Empire hopes that there might be some common ground where we are all enabled to stand together in such a way that our differences do not matter, to reduce Jesus to just another option in the Empire's "marketplace of ideas." So we are urged to suppress our concrete particularities in favor of more allegedly universal values. Caesar has always found it difficult to rule people who answer to stories other than those officially sanctioned by Caesar.

During the Gulf War, a student at a conservative evangelical seminary wrote me that, as a Bible-believing evangelical Christian, he could not figure out what we were doing killing people who have not heard the gospel of Jesus Christ. Evangelical Christians are supposed to believe that preaching the "name of Jesus" can change everything, even Iraqis.

I thought he was exactly right. What if, instead of cozying up to the president, Dr. Billy Graham had said, "George, give me a month to have a crusade in Baghdad. I think I can turn this thing around." When the president responded that he was not being "realistic," Dr. Graham could have told him about a counterreality called the kingdom of God, a kingdom that takes shape in speaking rather than killing.

Because we did not do this, because we forsook gospel foolishness for worldly wisdom, we never gave Iraq a chance to believe. Perhaps equally tragic, we did not give *ourselves* a chance to believe that Jesus Christ really is Lord. We exchanged our story for Caesar's and thereby forfeited our ability to preach the gospel in Iraq. People do not hear the gospel preached by people who are willing to murder their children.

God send us more conservative, Bible-believing, evangelical Christians!

We will not relinquish our story in the interest of helping Caesar, be he a democratically elected emperor or not, to keep the Empire together. Our story tells us that in this suffering, truthful Jew from Nazareth, in all the particularity of his incarnation, we have seen the universal love of God. The world, even in its ignorance, is his world and he shall reign.

The toughest evangelistic task we have as preachers is not how to make Jesus make sense in a disbelieving modern world, but whether, when he meets us in our world, as we believe that he does, we will follow him or not. He does not force us to follow him any more than he forced everyone who heard Paul on the Areopagus to follow. That he does not force us to follow is testimony that his kingdom, unlike any other kingdom with which we are familiar, is built upon truth rather than force.

All of which reminds us of how this episode of evangelistic preaching in Athens ends. The account does not end with the defeat signified in verse 17:32 ("When they heard of the resurrection of the dead, some scoffed . . ."). Nor does it end even with the open-minded liberal willingness of the sceptics to "hear you again about this."

The episode ends in *baptism*. "But some of them joined him and became believers, including Dionysius the Areopagite and a woman named Damaris, and others with them" (17:34). The ultimate "proof" for the validity of this gospel is not its alleged universality or applicability, but the church, that countercultural community (which Luke indicates by the mere mention of a woman as part of that community) formed of people like Damaris. The test for our speech is not its recognition by the "wider world" but rather its evocation of the church, of the congregation of people like Dionysius and Damaris. The church is the visible, baptismally derived, very public sign that the news in Jesus Christ is good news indeed, good news for all.[6]

---

6. See the excellent discussion of these themes in Walter Brueggemann, *Interpretation and Obedience* (Minneapolis: Fortress, 1991).

4

Preaching as Politics

WILL Campbell tells a story about William Stringfellow. At a National Conference on Religion and Race in Chicago in 1963, Stringfellow began his address by saying, "The issue, the only *issue,* at this conference is baptism."[1] Most of the delegates were shocked to hear so "sectarian" a reference, thinking that an issue like racism could be solved merely by appeals to "brotherhood" or "justice." Christians know that such problems can only be addressed as *political* and therefore *ecclesial* problems. We Christians have no other way of solving such problems, or even of naming why behavior like racism is a problem, other than our baptism and the peculiar political entity baptism evokes called church. Whenever anyone asks us preachers to say something "political," we must first say *church,* or better, we say *baptism.* The baptismal creation of the church is what John Howard Yoder called "the original revolution," that is, God's "creation of a distinct community with its

1. Will D. Campbell, *Brother to a Dragonfly* (New York: Seabury Press, 1977), p. 230.

own deviant set of values and its coherent way of incarnating them."[2]

Political Responsibility

Of course, as soon as we begin to speak of the distinctiveness of the Christian community, its "deviant values," many American Christians are conditioned to cry "irresponsibility." Most of the blame for this prejudice against the sectarian ethics of theologians like Yoder can be attributed to the Niebuhrs and their successors who taught us to believe that, in a democracy where the people have power, Christians have a responsibility to "go public" with their ethical agenda, to generalize their ethical principles as much as possible, to help transform the society into a place that more closely resembles God's will for the social order. The only other option is irresponsible withdrawal.

It would take too long to refute this line of reasoning here (the task performed in my book with Stanley Hauerwas, *Resident Aliens* [Nashville: Abingdon, 1989]). For our purposes, let us note that baptism has no qualms about the church being an utterly "political" phenomenon. Baptism is a sign of the creation of a new kingdom, a visible, political reality called the church. The question is not whether or not the church shall engage in politics; the question is, In *what kind of politics* shall we engage? The church may find that, when urged to "act responsibly" within the present secular order, it may have some very peculiar (peculiar in the world's eyes) notions of what it means to be responsible. When Christians say "politics" we are not compelled first to say "democracy," or "justice." We are compelled first to say

2. John Howard Yoder, *The Politics of Jesus* (Grand Rapids: Eerdmans, 1972), p. 28.

"church." For us, the church is God's means of confronting the principalities and powers with a new people who are organized around utterly different modes of communion than those offered by the world. "Sect" as a dirty word applies more to the United States and its murderously defended boundaries than to the church, which recognizes no boundaries, borders, or kings since the whole world is God's world.

As Christians are busy reformulating another world than that given by the regnant order, we may be accused of being "other-worldly." We are not. We are a sign, a political statement, a very public demonstration that God's "other world" is fully at hand (Mark 1:15). This world is Christ's and he is determined to rule. Caesar, beware.

Christians are those who believe that the most responsible thing we can do for our world is to be the church. We fear withdrawal from Christ and his claims more than we fear withdrawal from the state's politics. The church has no interest in withdrawing from social responsibility. It simply refuses to buy into the structures of responsibility as defined by the state.

It is unfortunate that, when contemporary Christians think about the church and politics, we do so through categories supplied to us by Richard Niebuhr's *Christ and Culture* (who received them from Ernst Troeltsch). Niebuhr's argument is rigged in such a way as to ensure that the reader will decide that the most pluralistic and inclusive of his five options, "Christ Transforming Culture," will be embraced as the most faithful. Today, reading *Christ and Culture* one realizes how many of these mainline Protestant pretensions have dissipated in the intervening years. Niebuhr wrote in a time when mainline Protestantism still considered itself culturally significant enough to transform a whole society. After all, American society was "our" world. The "Christ" Niebuhr set against "culture" was one rendered by nineteenth-century European scholarship, a "Christ" who could optimistically change "culture" only because the culture has changed Christ, a Christ whose main significance lay in his social utility.

Few contemporary American Christians believe such imperialistic assumptions — other than a few mainline church bureaucrats lobbying Congress. In our present situation, we are better able to hear anew other words by Richard Niebuhr on the church and the world:

> The world has always been against the church, but there have been times when the world has been partially converted and when the churches lived with it in some measure of peace; there have been other times when the world was openly hostile, seeking to convert the church. We live, it is evident, in a time of hostility, when the church is imperiled not only by an external worldliness but by one that has established itself within the Christian camp. Our position is inside a church which has been on the retreat and which has made compromise with the enemy in thought, in organization, and in discipline.[3]

Later, reaching for the language of withdrawal himself, Niebuhr asserts, "Only a new withdrawal followed by a new aggression can save the church and restore it to the salt with which to savor society" (pp. 123f.).

One of the most oppressive aspects of living in a godless society — or at least one populated by "practical atheists" who live as if there were no God — is that politics becomes everything, modern humanity's only means of transcendence. Many have noted that a person's political allegiance, to the political left or right, is much more determinative of a person's stance on issues like abortion or nuclear power than a

---

3. H. Richard Niebuhr, *The Church against the World* (Chicago: Willett and Clarke, 1935), p. 1.

person's religious beliefs. Politics is our chief means of naming ourselves, of seeking out a suitable caucus group composed of people with desires similar to ours, then agitating for government fulfillment of those desires. The state is god and politics is its liturgy.

So Richard John Neuhaus says that "the churches' chief political contribution is to debunk the inflated importance of politics."[4] Unfortunately, most of our churches, of the left or of the right, have succumbed to the illusion that politics is the "real world" to which all else, including the world of the baptized, is instrumental. In the words of Neuhaus, "The 'equipment of the saints' (Eph. 4) has been replaced by the recruitment of saints for our favored causes." When it comes to politics, today's church resembles nothing so much as a poor palsied nurse beside the culture's deathbed, mumbling words of comfort as this society disintegrates.

Aristotle defined politics as the creation of a *polis,* a city where it was safe to dwell because people were better because of their citizenship in the *polis* than they would have been if left to their own devices. Today, we use politics as the means whereby we cope with the loss of the *polis,* a means of pursuing self-interest, and of protecting ourselves against the omnivorous self-interest of others, in the absence of any motive for collaboration other than self-interest.

When politics is subsumed entirely under the state and then only as a means of securing individual rights and pursuing self-interest, the church is in danger of becoming just one more instrument in the vast network of state support, another agency where people come together to meet their needs, another means of the state keeping us focused upon ourselves rather than the society and its ills. In such a climate, the church is no longer salt or light. It is little more than a

4. Richard John Neuhaus, "Religion and Public Life: The Continuing Conversation," *The Christian Century,* July 11-18, 1990, p. 671.

gathering of those brought together by social class, race, gender, or other labels whereby the state manages its inhabitants, a moral uplift society, a group whose members share common aesthetics or therapeutic goals, a haven for the uncertain, a gathering for the dull.

Baptism stands as a visible reminder to the church that God has graciously called us for more. Baptism renders a savior who comes among us as one who infests our culture rather than is an inmate of it, a critic, judge, exorcist. He makes our fundamental categories, not "Christ and Culture" (Richard Niebuhr), but "Church and World" (Stanley Hauerwas). In so doing he demonstrates that his saving work is implacably political. He comes to call a new people, to evoke a new *polis* made by water and the Word. While I would in no way want to denigrate the importance of the cultic, liturgical character of the church, it is nevertheless interesting that most biblical language about Christ and his church (Messiah, kingdom, New Jerusalem, nation of priests, holy people) is far more political than cultic.

A Household as Witness

Luke gives us a glimpse of the peculiar political significance of the church. Luke 9:52-56 says that Jesus sent out messengers "to prepare for him" in unnamed Samaritan villages. This *hetoimazo* includes preparation for the hospitable reception of a stranger.[5]

A series of individuals come to Jesus, some requesting to follow him while others are asked by Jesus to follow (Luke 9:57-62). Jesus tells them that he and his followers can expect some inhospitable receptions along their way. For Jesus'

---

5. I am indebted for these insights to David P. Moessner, *Lord of the Banquet* (Minneapolis: Fortress, 1989), pp. 135-45.

people, the old laws are no longer in effect ("Leave the dead to bury their own dead"). Jesus' people are to focus only on their unique mission of proclamation ("But as for you, go and proclaim the kingdom of God").

All of this prepares us for Luke 10:1-24 and the mission of the "Seventy." These people are sent out on the same route Jesus himself will follow. Like those envoys sent into Samaria (Luke 9:52-56), they are forerunners of Jesus and therefore of his coming kingdom. Because the "harvest is plentiful," not even these Seventy (-two) will be enough. This urgent sending forth is for the purpose of gathering, forming a people of the kingdom. There is no "withdrawal" in any of this, but rather a sending forth, a sending forth into the world which will involve some peril. The nations are being gathered into a new kingdom, a gathering in which these emissaries are "like lambs into the midst of wolves." Despite this potentially dangerous situation, these ambassadors have the authority of "the Lord of the harvest."

Verses 4 through 6 indicate that they are to travel without provisions: no money, no nourishment, no extra clothing. These travelers will be totally dependent upon being received as guests in the homes along the way. In verses 5 and 6 the rationale for such measures is revealed. *The household (oikos), not the roadside, is to be the focus of their activity.* They are to speak "peace" when they enter a house (cf. Luke 19:42; Acts 10:36-37). This word of peace is none other than the very presence of the kingdom of God among them (verses 10-12). To reject the announcement of peace is to reject the kingdom and to have one's household abandoned. David Moessner shows that the household is both the starting point and the ultimate goal of these messengers' mission. Furthermore, *if the household does not receive the proclamation of peace, then the whole town is left desolate.* The kingdom has "drawn near," but not "upon them" (10:9, 11).

Curiously, once the messenger has been received into a

household, the messenger is to remain *in that house,* eating and drinking whatever is provided (10:7). This is not just a statement about the necessity for adequate pay for clergy! Here is the very goal of the mission of the Seventy. Their eating and drinking in this newfound house of peace is a sign of the eschatological kingdom. These meals represent the promised breaking of bread in the messianic banquet and thus the saving presence of the kingdom among us.

The injunction for these messengers not to move about from house to house (10:7) suggests that this eating and drinking is much more than simply providing meals for visiting preachers. If the main goal of this delegation were to evangelize as many homes as possible, then they would have been told not to tarry long at one household. Rather, the household itself represents the purpose of the sending of the Seventy. Verses 8 and 9 speak of *receiving* and *eating whatever is set before them,* followed by *healing* and *proclaiming* the presence of the kingdom. In being enjoined to eat "whatever is set before you," obviously the strict dietary laws for the Jew are not in effect. This suggests that the journeys of some of the Seventy may take them into fringe areas like Samaria where they may well be offered nonkosher food by the receiving household. So the sending of the Seventy is perhaps a foreshadowing of the day when the mission to Samaritans and Gentiles begins in earnest in Luke's second volume (Acts 8, 10). As Peter was to learn in Acts 10, eating and drinking becomes a powerful, very public (very political!) demonstration of the unity of Jew and Greek being wrought through baptism, as demonstrated in the house of Cornelius the gentile, the gentile army officer. (Who said the church did not want to threaten the political status quo?) No one, not even Ethiopian eunuchs or gentile army officers, is "unclean" in such a way that denies baptism, that hinders the church from boldly proclaiming the gospel.

The eating and drinking in these receptive households

becomes a sign of the presence of God, a sign of the promised messianic kingdom. Woe to those who will not receive, who will not eat and drink (verses 13-15).

So Jesus sends ambassadors ahead to prepare households for his arrival, to prepare people ready to eat and drink with Jesus when he arrives at their town (Luke 10:1). Urgency is necessitated because the Lord is already on his way. Evangelism here is not to cast the net as far as possible but rather to penetrate into marginal territory in order to ensure that some households will be prepared to show hospitality to Jesus. Households are needed that are willing to risk unconventional eating and drinking, in addition to healing and proclamation that will be for the good of the whole town.

Some of these evangelistic households will suffer rejection when no "sons of peace" (10:10-16) are found. Jesus is himself often rejected and some of the Seventy will similarly be rejected. The town's rejection of the emissaries and the households that respond to their peace greeting may at first seem to render these peace households irrelevant. The town may seek to discredit them by calling them "parochial," "irresponsible," "tribal," a "ghetto," or worse, a "sect." Such intended slurs will not trouble the household; they may even take them as compliments. Although the world may accuse these unique households of "withdrawal," their chief business is the very opposite of withdrawal. Their business is the very public, very social, very political one of *witness*, to be, in their unique eating and drinking, a sign of the kingdom, people preparing for the arrival of Jesus.

What good will a few odd households, a few reconstituted families do for the whole town? That is ultimately the Lord's problem. The sender of the laborers also promises a harvest. The Seventy return "with joy" (10:17), amazed that "even the demons" are subject to the name, the proclamation, the life together of this new people. The story ends in joy, as did so many of the meals with Jesus in Luke-Acts.

Escape from the Political to the Personal

Most of our inherited rites of baptism were heavily influenced by medieval baptismal liturgies that were themselves the result of a long process of the church's political accommodation. The Reformers, while calling for reform of the church, were amazingly content simply to transfer, with minor deletions, medieval baptismal rites into their Reformed churches. Perhaps they were able to do so because the Reformers, in their reform of the church, failed to raise the political question in such a way as to see the church as the gadfly of the state rather than its protectorate.

The secular political corruption of our baptismal theology shows up in the change in our theories of the atonement. We know that a number of theories of the atonement were operative in the early church. By the Middle Ages, however, satisfaction theories of the atonement had carried the day, and they were directly related to the changed political situation of the church after Constantine. Once the church was no longer in a battle with real political enemies, once the Christian faith was no longer a matter of a few distinctive households in town (Luke 10:1-24) but rather the possession of the whole town, salvation became internalized and individualized. Sin no longer names those social and political forces, the "principalities and powers," that embattle us, but becomes associated with individual desires and actions. Jesus is no longer the victor over the powers, the traveler coming to challenge the whole town, but one who makes a personal sacrifice to ensure my personal destiny.

Stanley Hauerwas has shown how, prior to Constantine, Christians saw themselves confronted by hostile powers personified in those who persecuted the church. Christians assumed that salvation meant rescue from and defeat of those powers. In baptism, pre-Constantinian Christians knew that those powers were already defeated. This made possible their confident and joyful challenge to the pretensions of imperial Rome. In their baptism, individual Christians found themselves caught up in a grand drama of God's salvation of all creation. Salvation was cosmic, a victory that God was achieving in Christ throughout all creation, a restoration not just of an individual life, but of the whole world to himself. Discipleship was a great cosmic adventure, not an individual story. Thus the church becomes necessary for the salvation of the world, since, without the church, how can the world know its true salvation? Prior to Constantine, it was the church that made visible God's working in history. So the historic claim that outside the church there is no salvation is an epistemological claim. Salvation is not a confirmation of what we already know and experience. It is an initiation into a story that could not be known apart from the exemplification of lives of people in a particular community. Imperial Rome could kill the baptized, make of them martyrs, but it could not determine the meaning of their deaths. Only the church could tell that story.

In a way, Rome did triumph. It subsumed the Christian story under the Imperial Roman one. The church bought into the notion that we could further the kingdom of God by means of the power of this world. World wisdom (politics) was substituted for gospel foolishness (church). The Augustinian heavy stress upon personally inherited guilt of sin as the main problem encountered through baptism led to the wholesale adoption of infant baptism as the norm for baptism in the Western church. Baptism lost its character as initiation into a distinctive community and became a washing of inherited sin by individuals for individual salvation.

Aggravating this tendency toward the radical individualizing of the sacraments was, throughout Northern European Christendom, the *preoccupation with liturgy as text,* a change stimulated by the invention of printing. Like Scripture's transformation from story into text, the liturgy was transformed from enactment into recitation. Literacy became the chief

105

Christian virtue. The God who was previously approached only through burning bushes, tombs, wombs, bread and wine, was now encountered through linear texts, available to all with the invention of the cheap book, which could be read, like all books, alone rather than with a group. The rites of the church, as embodied and enacted in the congregation, became a kind of obstacle for the new textual piety. (Parallels could be cited in the rise of textual, and later, so-called "higher" criticism of Scripture.) Once the embodied, enacted rite receded, so did the need for the gathered assembly at worship. In most Protestant liturgies, the didactic replaced the enacted. The truth was now thought to reside in the text, no longer in the implements, elements, and the participants in the liturgy. The worship of the church was transformed from a rather disordered, locally distinctive communal affair into a matter that could be centrally administered through church bureaucrats. Worship was constricted to a set of texts and Christian life became confrontation with certain words.

One of the major results of this textual preoccupation was the *depoliticizing of the liturgy*. Virtually gone from the church was the political sense that worship constitutes a new people, that it gathers together (*synagoge,* synagogue) and calls forth (*ekklesia,* church) a distinctive community, those households of peace in Luke 10. Liturgical study meant explication of texts. Biblical criticism meant peeling away the accumulated communal layers of interpretation to get back to "what the text originally meant." In both enterprises, the gathered community at worship was seen as an obstacle rather than the origin and purpose of the texts. The political function of the liturgy as the form of our life together as Christians was lost as the rites spoke to troubled individuals, reassuring them of cleansing from individual sins to make them fit for individual salvation.

While the Reformers were guilty of following the Augustinian stress on baptism as mainly a means of washing the individual's sins, Calvin defined baptism as "the sign of initiation by which we are received into the society of the church, in order that, engrafted in Christ, we may be reckoned among God's children" (*Institutes,* IV, 15, 1). Calvin's covenant theology helped him to retain a sense of baptism as initiation. Fortunately, new rites of baptism, in nearly all the churches, work to overcome the medieval (and Reformation) liturgies' almost exclusive emphasis on baptism as washing of personal sin and to restore baptism as Christian initiation. In other words, there is a new "political" emphasis in these rites. That political emphasis is the formation of a new *polis:*

> The first and most important implication of baptism is the formation of a diacritical community, the church. Baptism initiates the individual into a community that takes its identity from the death and resurrection of Christ. With a new identity, the Christian is reoriented to the world.[6]

All of the church's worship, including baptism, is the communal assertion and therefore cultivation of an alternative construction of society. At what points the church's alternative construction of society leads to conflict with our nonbelieving neighbors depends, of course, upon the neighbors. We cannot, however, remove the basic political challenge posed by the church to all counterpolitical schemes. The church's political responsibility begins with our being responsive to the God who has called us in baptism and who has wrenched a group of modern individuals away from the grip of the Empire in order to make us a household.

I was visiting in a congregation where, during the service, the preacher indulged in a practice not dear to my heart, a "children's sermon." He called the boys and girls down front. Squatting at the chancel he began,

6. Robert E. Webber and Rodney Clapp, *People of the Truth* (San Francisco: Harper & Row, 1988), p. 75.

Boys and girls, today is Epiphany. Epiphany always falls on January 6, but today it falls on Sunday. Epiphany is a strange word which means "manifestation," "revelation." A favorite Epiphany story is found at the beginning of Matthew's Gospel. You know the story. It's the story of the Wise Men who came to Bethlehem to see the baby Jesus. But they weren't really "Wise Men" or even "Three Kings." The Bible calls them "Magi." Magi. That's where we get our word "magic." They were magicians, astrologers — the kind Mrs. Reagan uses. [No laughter in congregation.] They came "from the East," some people think from Persia. Where is Persia? [Silence. One child hesitantly ventures, "Iran?"] "Yes. Good. Iran. That's Persia but it's not all of Persia. What other modern countries were once Persia? [Finally, a child says, "Iraq?"] "Yes. Good! Iraq. One of my favorite stories was "The Other Wise Man." Have you ever heard that story? As I remember, that Wise Man, that Magi came from Baghdad, which is now the capital of Iraq. And Matthew says, these Magi, *these Iraqis, were the first to get an epiphany, the first to see and to worship the baby Jesus.*

I daresay for that congregation, that sweet little children's sermon was a surprising, discomforting epiphany. Once again, God was among us, but not on our terms. That sermon was preached on January 6, 1991, about a week before we bombed Baghdad. Here at the beginning of a new year — and a new war — the beginning of the most "Jewish" of all the Gospels reminded us of the cosmic claims of Christ. To be a Christian is to be someone who has dared to expose oneself and one's children to such stories that carry the danger that an epiphany leads to politics.

Without the church, Christians would have nowhere to stand. The basis of all our ethics is the assumption of the presence of a visible, countercultural community that enables us to stand against the powers of cultural conformity. The church gives us a power we would not have on our own, enables us to listen to stories of Magi, stories too subversive to be listened to alone. Every sermon is a potential act of social reconstruction, the constitution of a social reality, a hospitable, countercultural household that did not exist before the articulation of a text like Matthew 3.

When viewing humanity, Christian thinkers from Augustine to Reinhold Niebuhr have made heavy use of the concepts of the fall and original sin. They laid a theological doctrine over the biblical text itself (as in most Reformation and post-Reformation readings of Genesis 3 and Romans 5) that resulted in a deeply pessimistic account of human nature. By the time Niebuhr finished with his anthropology, not much was left for human effort other than an "impossible possibility," an ideal to be realized only "beyond history."

Niebuhr's pessimism is so thoroughgoing, perhaps, because he has little place for the church in his theology. His anthropology is developed as if baptism never happened and the church were not essential. Christian ethics could rightly be accused of idealism, romanticism, ethical heroism, or ethical nihilism (depending upon the particular species of self-deception at work in the practitioner) if they are devised outside of the church. All *truly* Christian ethical positions presuppose a baptized community that make those positions credible and possible.

Of course, all beliefs and ethical positions are similarly community dependent, even though adherents may not think of themselves as dependent upon a community for their ethics. The person who decries the particularity and ecclesially conditioned character of Christian ethics in favor of an ethic that is more "universal" or "rational" is still dependent upon a community of language and belief to tell him just who is being "reasonable" and what views and values shall be privileged with the designation "universal." In politics, the issue does not seem to be *if* our political goals and methods shall be communally derived, only whether the community that gives us our politics will be true or false.

To be baptized is to be someone who has had citizenship transferred from one dominion to another. Of course, simply living in a new kingdom does not mean that the old accents, practices, and habits that characterized our life in the old domain are eradicated. It means that we keep exploring — every sermon, every church board meeting, every time we pray, every day in the world — the significance of our baptism. In our church disputes, in the face of new challenges, in deliberating on how best to be faithful in this world, we will refer back to our baptism, continuing to explore the meaning of, "I have been baptized."

If in my stress upon the communal, ecclesial character of the salvation that Christian baptism offers, you hear a distinctly Wesleyan emphasis, I am pleased. In his classic essay "The Character of a Methodist" and elsewhere, John Wesley laid out an "Order of Salvation." Wesley's first step was to "awaken" in his hearers a knowledge of their need, a desire to "flee the wrath to come" and experience new life. Second, awakened people were invited to enroll in a Methodist "class meeting." Even if they had not yet understood or felt anything about their salvation, they were offered membership in these small groups of twelve or fewer people. The classes met weekly and provided a place for mutual study, correction, forgiveness, and prayer. If things went well in the small group, three months later they were invited to join a Methodist "society." How odd that Wesley should be thought of today as the forerunner of our thoroughly subjectivized pietism when he so thoroughly believed in Christianity as a matter of enculturation and initiation into a group.

It was expected that, in these groups, in God's good time and manner, the participants would experience justification. This appears to have happened, in the early Methodist socie-

110

ties, within a few months or years. This was the third step, the conviction that Jesus Christ had died for them and their sins and had made right their relationship to God.

Fourth, their groups encouraged the participants to expect an experience of entire sanctification, perfection by which their lives would be lived entirely according to God's will. While many early Methodists apparently never came to such an experience, the Wesleyan notion of perfection accounted for the distinctively ethical energy of the movement.

Wesleyans experienced the gospel call, not merely as the intellectual "Do you agree?" or the emotional "Do you feel?" but as the political "Will you join up?"

When Paul appeals to a squabbling congregation to get itself together by remembering who it is, you expect him to reach for a baptismal metaphor, and he does. Even as they have put on a new white garment in their baptism, so they are to "put on Christ":

> Then put on the garments that suit God's chosen people, his own, his beloved: compassion, kindness, humility, gentleness, patience. Be forbearing with one another, and forgiving where any of you has cause for complaint: you must forgive as the Lord forgave you. . . . Whatever you are doing, whether you speak or act, do everything in the name of the Lord Jesus, giving thanks to God the Father through him. (Colossians 3:12-17, NEB)

Most truly Christian ethics begin with a reminder of our adoption into this new household, a reminder of our baptism.

Faced with the seeming omnipotence of the Nazi state, Dietrich Bonhoeffer said that discipleship could not be a matter of withdrawing into inwardness. Withdrawal would never empower Christians to resist the world's opposition. The only hope for Christians in an alien world was membership in a community that would enable them to resist. As

Bonhoeffer told us, membership in that community made real Christian growth, sanctification, possible:

> There is a certain "political" character involved in the idea of sanctification and it is this character which provides the only basis for the Church's political ethic. The world is the world and the Church the Church, and yet the Word of God must go forth from the Church into all the world, proclaiming that the earth is the Lord's and all that therein is. Herein lies the "political" character of the Church.[7]

The Cultivation of a New People

Richard Niebuhr, in *Christ and Culture,* spoke of the ways in which something called "Christ" related to something called "Culture." Aside from whatever biblical reservations we might have about this entity so amorphously labeled as "Christ," we might also note the way in which Niebuhr used "culture."

Until the eighteenth century, culture was a noun that named a process, usually related to agriculture: the culture *of* something. Animal culture. Grape culture. Farmers were those who cultivated. The origin of "culture" goes back to the Latin *colere,* which meant to cultivate, to protect. It also relates, in Latin, to acts of worship. The word "cult," referring to liturgical actions, is related to the Latin root, *cultura.*[8]

During the sixteenth century, the notion of culture as a process of tending natural growth, cultivation, was extended to the more metaphorical meaning of human development. So Francis Bacon spoke of the need for "the culture and

---

7. Dietrich Bonhoeffer, *The Cost of Discipleship* (New York: Macmillan, 1959), p. 314.

8. My thanks to Dr. Steve Long for these reflections on the meanings of "culture."

manurance of minds" (1605). During the eighteenth and nineteenth centuries, "culture" came to be used as an abstract noun denoting the result of a social process. In Germany, *Kultur* became a synonym for "civilization," all that Germany prided itself on possessing as opposed to other uncivilized (that is, non-German) societies. From here, culture came to be associated with those practices relating particularly to intellectual or artistic life. A government's "Ministry of Culture" propagates artistic endeavor. Lately, we have worked to overcome the class distinctions and implicit claims of superiority implied in the word "culture" by stressing "cultural pluralism." The world is made up, not of culture as opposed to barbarism, but of many different cultures, with one culture not necessarily superior to another. Currently, at the university where I teach, a great deal is being made of the positive value of "multicultural diversity." By stressing the equality of "cultures," those groups who have previously been silenced or ignored by the dominant social group hope to get a voice within the society.

Where such descriptions of human groupings are used, it seems fair for Christians to admit that we also are a culture. When Richard Niebuhr was describing "Christ and Culture," he was not really describing two utterly different entities, culture in opposition to some phenomenon ("Christ") that was not a culture. He was describing two different cultures. Christianity can be described as a culture, a set of practices, beliefs, a distinctive language.

The oddness of Christianity as a culture that ran counter to the surrounding Roman culture was well appreciated by its first converts. Justin Martyr, taking up the biblical language about beating swords into plowshares, says that, "whereas we once cultivated the arts of war, we now cultivate righteousness and peace." The image was a felicitous one. According to Justin, those who once cultivated (even as farmers cultivate with plows) war, now cultivate peace. Christianity requires cultivation, the long-term development of those skills, languages, and practices necessary for this culture.

We must learn Christianity, even as we learn a foreign language. The task of the Christian preacher is not so much to evoke what is already there, incipient in every human being. The task of preaching is to teach what would not be known before it is announced, to cultivate those insights, means of describing, and vocabulary with which Christians describe the world. Preaching is therefore always somewhat out beyond the congregation, always destabilizing, beckoning, reconstructing the taken-for-granted world of the present. So much of Jesus' preaching, and the best of our own, is eschatological, an announcement of an end to the present order so that God can have room to make a new one.

Perhaps cultivation was easier when Christianity was embraced by a greater percentage of the population in the surrounding society. I doubt it. When the surrounding society claims to be "Christian," perhaps the possibilities for misunderstanding and misrepresentation of the gospel are even greater.

My friend Rick Edens was visiting in Soviet Georgia. A Georgian Baptist was showing him his church. "To be a Christian here, to be baptized, is to be motherless," said the man. "When one comes up out of the water, one has lost country, parents, all."

Today, there is a much clearer sense that Christians in our society function as a minority, a subculture within a larger culture that is not Christian. There is therefore a new awareness that Christian communicators must take seriously their task as cultivators, among the baptized, of Christian consciousness. Disciples are not born. They are made through baptism and teaching (Matthew 28:19-20).

The baptized, through the preaching of the church, continue to explore the meaning of their adoption into a new people, the *polis* of God created and cultivated by water and the Word. In the words of a fifth-century inscription, perhaps written by Leo the Great (c. 461) in the Lateran Baptistry,

> Here is born in Spirit-soaked fertility
> a brood destined for another City,
> begotten by God's blowing
> and borne upon this torrent
> by the Church their virgin mother.
> Reborn in these depths they reach for heaven's realm,
> the born-but-once unknown by felicity.
> The spring is life that floods the world,
> the wounds of Christ is awesome source.
> Sinner sink beneath this sacred surf
> that swallows age and spits up youth.
> Sinner here scour sin away down to innocence,
> for they know no enmity who are by
> one font, one Spirit, one faith made one.
> Sinner shudder not at sin's kind and number,
> for those born here are holy.[9]

9. Quoted in Aidan Kavanagh, *The Shape of Baptism: The Rite of Christian Initiation* (New York: Pueblo, 1978), p. 49.

"The New Family"

The Fifth Sunday after Easter
Acts 8:26-40

An angel of the Lord said to Philip, "Rise and go toward the south to the road that goes down from Jerusalem to Gaza." This is a desert road. And he rose and went. And behold, an Ethiopian, a eunuch, . . . had come to Jerusalem to worship. (Acts 8:26-27)

SOME time ago I wrote an article, in a church publication, criticizing my own denomination's infatuation with racial, gender, and ethnic quotas. So many Asian women for this committee, Native Americans for that board. I don't like quotas. I don't mind them for the government; after all, I see no way for the government to work justice other than legalistic means such as ethnic and gender quotas. But in the church, I argued, we shouldn't need quotas to force us to do right.

I received a long letter from a person in Kansas. She thanked me for my article, then she took me to task. At eighteen, she felt called by God to the Christian ministry. She wanted to go be a minister to small congregations in rural Kansas. She began, even at eighteen, to prepare herself, majoring in religion in college.

She is now twenty-eight. Ten years of prayer, preparation, and expectation later, she is not a minister. Her denomination does not ordain women.

In her letter she said, "What you say about the church not judging people by labels of black, white, male, female may be good, but I can tell you, from bitter experience, the church does judge people that way, with the same labels by which the world judges people. I don't think it will ever change."

We are now five Sundays after Easter, that day, that bright Sunday morning when once dead Jesus burst the bonds of death and came forth from the tomb. Life stepped over the boundary of death. The impossible, inconceivable happened, and the future was cracked open with fresh potential.

But five Sundays from Easter is a long time. And we get back from the cemetery, the sound of Easter trumpets fades away, and we wonder what, if anything, really changed.

Eventually, the old boundaries fall back into place. The Easter sun goes down. The sun rises again on Monday and it's the same old sun, the same old world, the same old you, the same old me. The Fifth Sunday of Easter is a long way from Easter.

And the deadly boundaries seem so impervious, so impenetrable to the assaults of a living, let-loose Easter Savior. And sometimes the most insidious boundaries are the ones we love the most, the boundaries that provide us such comfortable identity, such sure space that we don't even know they are boundaries, we don't see how confined we are behind the barriers.

Take the family, for instance. If there is one human experience dear to us, it is our family. We love our families. During the last presidential election, protection for and funding in behalf of the family became a major political concern. Family was the one issue a politician could be for without stepping on anyone's toes.

Indeed, it is difficult to imagine a more cherished human

117

arrangement than the family. We would die for our families, even kill for them. Most of us are not violent by nature. And yet when asked, "If your family were threatened, your children, would you kill someone if it were necessary to protect your family?" the majority of us would readily answer, "Yes."

There appears to be no limit to our love for our family, even murder.

Blood is thicker than water. Our family is the source of our name, our values. Home is where you go when you have absolutely nowhere else to go. Family are the people who take you in when everyone else has rejected you. And the church is praised as an institution that is so helpful in support of the family. Churches have "Family Night Suppers," and they build "Family Life Centers," much larger than their sanctuaries. We even have churches that advertise that they are a "Family Church."

In fact, I found in my last church that perhaps the major reason people give for joining a church is support of their family. New members ask a church, "What can you do for my family?"

We have thereby papered over, indeed forgotten, how deeply ambiguous, even negative, the early church was about family. In his book *The First Urban Christians,* Wayne Meeks notes that pagan Roman society had no more cherished value than its belief in the primacy of the family. Every Roman institution had its basis in the Roman family. There was no means of social advancement (other than the military) in ancient Rome other than marriage into a more superior family, because your family determined your status in life.

A major Roman criticism of Christians was that Christians destroyed the family. I remember a preacher here in Duke Chapel preaching on Jesus' calling of his disciples, telling the story of the calling of the sons of Zebedee, how they left their father with the fishing nets and followed Jesus. The story doesn't say what their father thought about his two sons walking out of the family business and tagging along after this itinerant rabbi named Jesus. The story doesn't care. And the preacher commented, "Jesus broke the hearts of many a first-century family."

Stanley Hauerwas opens one of his classes by reading a letter from a parent to a government official. The parent complains that his son, who had received the best education, gone to all the right schools, and was headed for a good job as a lawyer, had gotten involved with a weird religious sect. Now members of this sect controlled his every move, told him whom to date and whom not to date, and had taken all of his money. The parent is pleading with the government official to do something about this weird religious group.

"Who is this letter describing?" Hauerwas asks. Some think it is describing the Moonies, or some other weird sect.

It is a composite letter drawn from the letters of third-century Roman parents concerning a group called the church.

Once they came to Jesus, saying, "Your mother and brothers are outside asking for you."

"Who are my mother, my brothers?" asked Jesus. His family was that new gathering of people called disciples.

The family is the source not only of our greatest gifts but also of our greatest damage. I doubt that when psychiatrists are counseling deeply troubled persons, they talk about much other than family. The family has become the one, the only place of our identity and direction, the only place in our lives where there are people who care for us and know us. This has led to a kind of tyranny of the family. Lacking any institutions within our lives with the power to stand against the family, bereft of any other source of identity or meaning, the family takes over everything. The sad state of many American families may be testimony to the truth, not that we don't love our families, but that we love them too much. We are asking our families to bear far too much moral and spiritual weight, to be all things for us, and they crack under the strain.

I have decided, since coming here to the university and working with young people, that one of the greatest gifts a parent can give a child is the reassurance that all of the parent's hopes, dreams, and aspirations are not resting upon that child. Whenever the parent complains to the child that, "I gave you. . . ," "You owe me. . . ," the family has failed. And one of the greatest gifts children can give parents is the reassurance that the source and significance of their lives is not totally dependent upon the competency or goodness of the parents.

The family appears to be one of those human arrangements that is dependent upon other secure human arrangements in order to survive and in order not to become demonic and destructive.

Most of the really serious damage that is done to us occurs in family. The blood of the family is thicker and more indelible than any other attachment in our lives.

And if you're not in a family, then you're apt to be very, very lonely, for we live in a society in which family is the one, the only attachment that matters. Show me a church that builds a "Single Life Building."

It was after Easter, five weeks after Easter, to be exact. Philip is sleeping and awakens suddenly to find an angel standing before him. "Get up!" says the angel, and go out into the middle of the desert at noon.

And out in the desert he meets a man. Is it a man? He is a eunuch, a chamberlain in the court of the queen of the Ethiopians, Candace. He is returning from a visit to the temple in Jerusalem and he is reading an Isaiah scroll.

And he has come to that passage from Isaiah: "He was led like a lamb to the slaughter, like a sheep before its shearers is dumb. He didn't open his mouth. Justice was

120

denied him. He has been cut off from the land of the living. Who is going to declare his posterity?"

Who is going to declare his posterity? This man will never have any posterity because he has been "cut off." He is without generation.

Who is that? When Philip climbs up into the Ethiopian's chariot, that is the eunuch's first question. "Who is that?" Who is that?" Is the prophet talking about himself or somebody else?

Why is this man so interested in this obscure passage from Isaiah?

He is a eunuch. And the Scripture says quite plainly, as plain as the nose on your face, Deuteronomy 23:1, that the eunuch "shall not enter the assembly of the Lord."

There shall be no place in God's family for a eunuch. He will never have a family, this sexless person by accident, or choice, or royal decree. Throughout Scripture children are praised as a reward of God, a sign of divine blessing. But this eunuch will never have children, will never have a family and therefore will have no place in the family of God. He can never enter the temple and praise God with the rest of us who have been blessed by God with family.

This eunuch is reading this passage in Isaiah. Who is this who is cut off, cut off from the land of the living, without posterity, therefore without future? Who is this? Is this the prophet or is this someone else?

Because the prophet Isaiah says, "The days will come when the foreigner will no longer say, 'The Lord will separate me from his people.' The days will come when the eunuch will no longer say, 'O I am just a dry stick.' The days will come when the eunuch who loves me and my house and my covenant shall have a name written in my house and my covenant which shall be better than a thousand sons and daughters and will be remembered forever."

This man has been up to Jerusalem foraging around in

the Bible trying to find his name. He has been up to Jerusalem but they won't let him in. The Bible says clearly, "Don't let him in." (Thanks to Fred Craddock for this insight.)

Has any of you gone to church and been made to stand outside? Have you gone to worship where you are not welcome, stand, all during the service, peering in, hoping to hear just a snippet of the prayers? Standing on the outside, excluded.

Have you ever been to church, or been listening to Scripture, and had to stand outside?

And now he has at last found a place in the Bible that offers hope, a passage that may be speaking to him.

"Who is this?" he asks Philip.

"Why, that was Jesus of Nazareth," says Philip. "He was cut off. He had no family, no issue, and yet *he created the largest family in the world.*"

"What is to forbid me from joining the family? Can I too be adopted, baptized?"

Philip said, "Well, er, uh, I might baptize you, but here in the desert, there's no water."

"Look," exclaimed the eunuch, "here is water"!

And Philip sighed and muttered to himself, "They were upset at First Church Jerusalem when I baptized those Samaritans (Acts 8:4-25). They're gonna' kill me for this."

And right there, in the desert, a white man and a black man, a Jew and an Ethiopian, Philip baptized the eunuch. There was water in the desert.

In *this* new family, water is thicker than blood.

Index of Names